The Spirit Said Go

Lessons in Guidance from Paul's Journeys

The Spirit Said Go

Lessons in Guidance from Paul's Journeys

MARK WILSON

WIPF & STOCK · Eugene, Oregon

THE SPIRIT SAID GO
Lessons in Guidance from Paul's Journeys

Wipf & Stock
An Imprint of Wipf and Stock Publishers
199 W. 8th Ave., Suite 3
Eugene, OR 97401

www.wipfandstock.com

PAPERBACK ISBN: 978-1-5326-3013-2
HARDCOVER ISBN: 978-1-5326-3015-6
EBOOK ISBN: 978-1-5326-3014-9

Manufactured in the U.S.A.   09/06/17

To our children

Leilani and her husband Erik,

Winema and her husband Eric,

Jim,

David and his wife Heather,

and our grandchildren

Ezra, Zebulon, Lila, Simeon,

Nathan, Jordan, Bethany, and Vivienne,

who have made this journey with us.

We apologize for the detours and missed roads,

and pray that we all reach the same destination.

Contents

Introduction | ix
Contributing Friends and Colleagues | xiii

1 The Journey to Damascus
    Lesson 1: God uses his sovereignty to guide us before we are believers. | 2

2 The Early Journeys
    Lesson 2: God uses spiritual mentors to guide us. | 8
    Lesson 3: God uses prophets to guide us. | 14

3 The First Journey
    Lesson 4: God uses church leaders to guide us. | 20
    Lesson 5: God uses human networks to guide us. | 25
    Lesson 6: God uses providential encounters to guide us. | 29
    Lesson 7: God uses adversity to guide us. | 36
    Lesson 8: God uses a sense of duty to guide us. | 43

4 The Second Journey
    Lesson 9: God uses conflict to guide us. | 50
    Lesson 10: God uses closed doors to guide us. | 56
    Lesson 11: God uses visions and dreams to guide us. | 63

5 The Third Journey
    Lesson 12: God uses open doors to guide us. | 70
    Lesson 13: God uses Spirit-led decision making to guide us. | 76
    Lesson 14: God uses changed circumstances to guide us. | 84
    Lesson 15: God uses the compulsion of the Spirit to guide us. | 91
    Lesson 16: God uses personal prophecy to guide us. | 98

6 The Journey to Jerusalem and Caesarea

    Lesson 17: God uses our religious, civic, and national identities
        to guide us. | 106

7 The Journey to Rome

    Lesson 18: God uses faulty decision making to guide us. | 116
    Lesson 19: God uses angels to guide us. | 122
    Lesson 20: God uses fellow believers to guide us. | 128

8 Our Journeys in Guidance | 135

Appendix 1: Additional Examples of Guidance in Acts | 137
Appendix 2: From Peyote Way to Jesus Way | 139
Appendix 3: The Night I Met the Devil | 142
Appendix 4: The Fountainhead Prophecy by Dick Eastman | 146
Appendix 5: Prophecy Today | 147

Bibliography | 149

Introduction

Over forty years ago on Mother's Day in 1974 my wife Dindy and I began our new life in Christ. God has enabled us to live this journey of faith in an unusual but productive way. This book celebrates our pilgrimage while sharing some of the lessons in guidance learned along the way. It also introduces Paul's own journeys and the various ways the apostle was guided as he proclaimed the gospel. My numerous travels along the routes recorded in Acts, sometimes experiencing guidance at the same sites, likewise provided insights into this subject.

Who are we, and what caused me to write a book on guidance? My wife Dindy (given name Elinda) was born into a Jewish home and grew up on the Upper West Side of Manhattan in New York City. I was raised in a small town in North Dakota, whose inhabitants numbered fewer than the occupants in her apartment building. Dindy thinks that I grew up in a "Leave It to Beaver" kind of setting. My father worked for the Soo Line Railroad, and for the first ten years of my life our family lived above the train depot in Fullerton, North Dakota. Instead of hunting pheasants and waterfowl in the wide-open prairies as I did, Dindy rode her bike in Central Park and played hopscotch on 92nd Street. Because of such diverse backgrounds, we jokingly say that we have a cross-cultural marriage and consider it a miracle that we even met. The story of our meeting in a tipi on a hippie commune in Colorado, how we became believers during a peyote meeting with Native Americans in South Dakota, and other personal vignettes as they relate to God's guidance will be told in this book (see particularly Appendix 2).

My interest in divine guidance began early in my Christian walk as I desired to find God's will in every area of my life (cf. 1 Thess 5:18; 1 Pet 2:15). While attending Christ for the Nations Institute in Dallas, I became greatly influenced by the teaching of the Pentecostal author Donald Gee.

Introduction

This book's title is derived in part from Gee's book, *Studies in Guidance*.[1] A book on guidance that also influenced me was Garry Friesen's *Decision Making and the Will of God*. Friesen's perspective liberated me from always trying to find one "perfect" path and helped me to realize that God gave me free will to explore a range of options that are "good and pleasing" to him (Rom 12:2). This has allowed me to think outside the traditional guidance box and to make bold decisions while pursuing God's will for our lives.

When I worked for the Christian Broadcasting Network in the 1990s, I was involved in a discipleship curriculum project called *Living By The Book*. One of its courses was "Guidance By The Book," which featured the teaching of Dr. M. Blaine Smith, a specialist on the subject. Working with Blaine and reading his book *Knowing God's Will* greatly expanded my theological and practical understanding of guidance. Blaine has graciously allowed me to use an excerpt from that volume.

Before leaving Tulsa, Oklahoma, in 2001, I preached a sermon at Believers Church on guidance in the book of Acts. This initial foray into the topic whetted my interest to develop it further; however, the timing was not right for writing a book. The Lord knew there were many additional lessons to learn. Although Dindy and I had both visited Turkey multiple times including a four-month stay in 2001, it was not until 2004 that we moved to Turkey permanently. So for over a decade I have gained further insights living in the land where Paul's journeys took place. It has been my privilege to travel to most of the places in the eastern Mediterranean mentioned in the book of Acts and to journey along the ancient roads and routes upon which Paul traveled.

My initial academic writing on this subject was published in a 2005 article.[2] I later wrote briefly about guidance in a devotion for a volume edited by my friend Verlyn Verbrugge†.[3] In recent years I have taught this material in Christian education classes and in sermons at the Saint Paul Union Church in Antalya. I have also taught about Acts and guidance for the Discipleship Beyond program held annually in Antalya. Seeing how this material benefitted other believers trying to understand divine guidance was a further impetus to bring this book to fruition.

A word about the title: The first verb in Jesus' commission to the disciples in Matthew 28:19 is "Go." Following his ascension in Acts, Jesus

---

1. On Gee's approach see my article, "Studies in Guidance."
2. Wilson, "Role of the Holy Spirit."
3. Wilson, "Paul: Bound in the Spirit."

similarly commanded his disciples to go and be witnesses in Jerusalem, Judea, Samaria, and to the ends of the earth (1:8). In Acts 1–12 Peter is the primary witness; in chapters 13–28 Paul is that witness. Along the way the Spirit sometimes said "Wait" or "No" to them, but this was always while they were in the act of going. I firmly believe that all Christians are still called to "Go." All guidance we receive today is ultimately part of that same commission to be witnesses to Jesus wherever he has placed us.

This book is unusual in that it is both inductive Bible study and spiritual (auto)biography. The most productive way to experience each lesson is to: 1) read the target scripture at its beginning, 2) read the larger context of that passage in Acts, 3) read my comments on Paul's guidance, 4) read the examples of guidance today, and lastly 5) read and engage with the reflection questions. In this way you will get the most out of reading the book. Most of all, enjoy especially the "Guidance Today" sections because they celebrate God's faithfulness in the life of each contributor.

The historical and archaeological background of Paul's journeys in Acts has been a focus of my ongoing research and writing. The maps at the beginning of each chapter will help orient you to the geography of that journey. For further archaeological details related to the book, see my contribution on "Acts" in the *ESV Archaeology Bible*. Specific site and travel information is usually drawn from articles mentioned in the notes and available to read or download from my pages on www.academia.edu. Unless otherwise noted, all scriptures are drawn from Acts. Additional examples of guidance in Acts, apart from Paul and his journeys, are found in Appendix 1.

The maps were created especially for this book by Sinan Özşahinler of Tutku Tours in Izmir, Turkey. I want to thank Tutku's owner, Levent Oral, for his assistance in creating these maps.

One final caveat: the text reflects my own views and opinions and should not be construed to represent those of the friends and colleagues who graciously contributed reflections of their own experiences of divine guidance. Many others have made significant input into our lives through this journey, and I apologize in advance to each that you and your special contribution could not be mentioned in the book due to lack of space. Yet you are not forgotten either by us or the Lord.

Antalya, Turkey
Mother's Day, May 14, 2017

Contributing Friends and Colleagues

James Bultema: Founder of the St. Paul Cultural Center and emeritus pastor of the St. Paul Union Church, Antalya, Turkey.

Bill Cash: Itinerant sailor and classmate at Christ for the Nations Institute, living in New Jersey.

Jackson Crum: Pastor of the Park Community Church in Chicago, Illinois, and occasional summer preacher at the St. Paul Union Church.

Timothy George: Dean of the Beeson Divinity School and Professor Divinity History and Doctrine at Samford University, Birmingham, Alabama.

Anna Griffith: Fellow traveler on the BAS Egnatian Way tour in 2015, living in Texas.

Dan Gutierrez: Outreach Director, Discipleship Beyond, Antalya, Turkey.

Cyndy Holter: Grief Chaplain at Restoration Coaching, living in Texas.

Michael Holter: Gifted artist and fellow North Dakotan (like Cyndy), living in Texas.

Eugene Jahn: Accountant for our two nonprofit organizations and president of Eugene Jahn and Associates, living in Colorado.

Dennis Massaro: Senior pastor of the St. Paul Union Church, Antalya, Turkey.

Marius Nel: Associate Professor of New Testament Studies, Stellenbosch University, Stellenbosch, South Africa.

Contributing Friends and Colleagues

Mark D. Roberts: Executive Director of the Max De Pree Center for Leadership, Fuller Seminary, Pasadena, California.

Katherine Rutt: Financial assistant and support administrator for our two nonprofit organizations, living in Virginia.

Jonathan Shirey: Founder and Director, Discipleship Beyond, Antalya, Turkey.

M. Blaine Smith: Founder of Nehemiah Ministries, living in Maryland.

Sam Storms: Lead pastor at Bridgeway Church, Oklahoma City, OK, and president of Enjoying God Ministries.

Linford Stutsman: Professor of Religion, Eastern Mennonite University, Harrisonburg, VA, and director of the SailingActs program.

Ed Vinieratos: Fellow traveler to Israel in 2015, living in Latvia.

Dindy Wilson: Faithful, believing wife who has shared this journey with me.

1

The Journey to Damascus

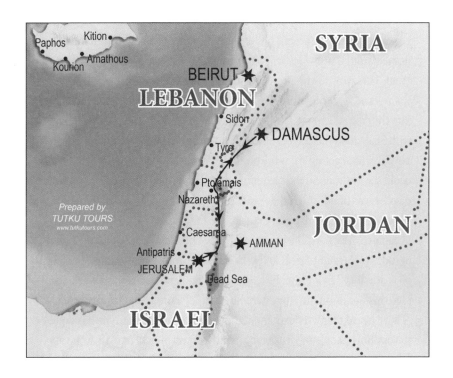

Lesson 1

God uses his sovereignty to guide us before we are believers.

³ As Saul neared Damascus on his journey, suddenly a light from heaven flashed around him. ⁴ He fell to the ground and heard a voice say to him, "Saul, Saul, why do you persecute me?" ⁵ "Who are you, Lord?" Saul asked. "I am Jesus, whom you are persecuting," he replied. ⁶ "Now get up and go into the city, and you will be told what you must do." ⁷ The men traveling with Saul stood there speechless; they heard the sound but did not see anyone. ⁸ Saul got up from the ground, but when he opened his eyes he could see nothing. So they led him by the hand into Damascus. ⁹ For three days he was blind, and did not eat or drink anything. ¹⁰ In Damascus there was a disciple named Ananias. The Lord called to him in a vision, "Ananias!" "Yes, Lord," he answered. ¹¹ The Lord told him, "Go to the house of Judas on Straight Street and ask for a man from Tarsus named Saul, for he is praying. ¹² In a vision he has seen a man named Ananias come and place his hands on him to restore his sight." ¹³ "Lord," Ananias answered, "I have heard many reports about this man and all the harm he has done to your holy people in Jerusalem. ¹⁴ And he has come here with authority from the chief priests to arrest all who call on your name." ¹⁵ But the Lord said to Ananias, "Go! This man is my chosen instrument to proclaim my name to the Gentiles and their kings and to the people of Israel. ¹⁶ I will show him how much he must suffer for my name." ¹⁷ Then Ananias went to the house and entered it. Placing his hands on Saul, he said, "Brother Saul, the Lord—Jesus, who appeared to you on the road as you were

coming here—has sent me so that you may see again and be filled with the Holy Spirit." [18] Immediately, something like scales fell from Saul's eyes, and he could see again. He got up and was baptized, [19] and after taking some food, he regained his strength. (9:3–19)

Paul's Guidance

The conversion of Paul[1] while journeying to Damascus is so foundational to his life and ministry that our discussion of guidance must begin here. This emphasis is also found in Acts. In chapter 9 Luke describes Paul's conversion experience. Then in chapter 22 before the Jews in Jerusalem and in chapter 26 before the Roman governor Festus, King Agrippa, and Queen Bernice in Caesarea, Paul himself described his conversion. Also, on his first visit to Jerusalem after his conversion Paul told his story to the apostles (9:27). The fourfold repetition of Paul's conversion in Acts emphasizes its importance.

The motive for Paul's Damascus journey was nefarious: he wanted to "neutralize" the followers of the Way there, as Stephen had been. But outside the city a divine intervention occurred, and Paul was struck to the ground. In the three extended accounts several elements are repeated:

1. Paul was authorized by the Jewish authorities in Jerusalem to punish the followers of Jesus (9:2; 22:5; 26:12).

2. While approaching Damascus, Paul saw a light and heard a voice (9:3–4; 22:6–7; 26:13–14).

3. The voice asked, "Saul, Saul, why do you persecute me?" (9:4; 22:7; 26:14).

4. Paul answered, "Who are you, sir/lord?" (9:5; 22:8; 26:15).

5. The voice replied, "I am Jesus, whom you are persecuting" (9:5; 22:8; 26:15).

After introducing himself, Jesus then gave Paul a word of guidance: he was to continue into the city where he would be told what to do. In Damascus Paul fasted for three days and awaited further directions. Simultaneously, Jesus also prepared a disciple in Damascus to give Paul further

---

1. Although Luke uses his Jewish name Saul until 13:9, his Roman name Paul is generally used in this volume. Such usage is not meant to minimize his Jewish background in any way.

instructions. In a vision Ananias was told to go to a specific house on Straight Street—that of Judas—where he would find the blinded Paul of Tarsus. Then he was to lay hands on him so Paul's sight could be restored. Ananias's initial reaction to the vision was normal: he was fearful because he had heard rumors about Paul's harmful intentions. After being reassured that this man was a chosen instrument of God, Ananias found Paul and prayed for him. Not only was Paul's eyesight miraculously restored, but he was also filled with the Holy Spirit and baptized in water. Both were the shared spiritual experiences that characterized new believers in the early church (see 2:41; 4:31; 8:12, 17, 38).

An immediate consequence of Paul's experience was that he was now one of "them"—the disciples of Jesus. As he argued in the synagogue that Jesus was the Son of God, Jewish opponents plotted to kill him. This is the first of many occasions in Acts where Paul was forced to flee from a city in order to save his life (9:20–25).

Despite wrong motives and evil plans against Jesus and the early church, God sovereignly orchestrated the circumstance (the journey) and the individual (Ananias), which led to Paul's conversion and initiation into the kingdom of God. He learned that Jesus had a divine plan at work for his life even before he acknowledged him as Lord. Paul's initial experience with Jesus on his journey to Damascus no doubt also brought an expectation of divine guidance in the future. Is it any wonder that Paul repeatedly received such guidance during his subsequent journeys?

Guidance Today

It was a mild spring morning in 1974 in the Badlands region of the Pine Ridge Indian Reservation in southwestern South Dakota. The Native American Church (NAC) meeting that Dindy and I were attending had reached the moment in its all-night ritual when the break for morning water took place. The occasion was Mother's Day (see Appendix 2 for the background). Through a series of encounters and experiences over the previous months, God had been sovereignly preparing us for the surprising turn of events to occur early that day.

I was serving that night as the fireman for the service, assisting my friend Emerson who was leading it in his office as high priest of the church in South Dakota. Peyote is derived from a cactus that grows along the Rio Grande River in southern Texas and northern Mexico. I visited these peyote "gardens" once while accompanying my Lakota friends to purchase peyote for meetings. Peyote's active alkaloid is a natural hallucinogen called mescaline. Among Native Americans peyote is legal to use within a religious context. As a kind of a deacon, I was responsible for keeping the fire in the center aglow for ceremonial use. Around four o'clock that morning I had prepared the bucket of water with a ladle that would be passed around for refreshment during the morning break. After the staff and eagle feathers had passed back to Emerson at the head of the circle, he signaled that I should bring in the water.

He began to sing a peyote song in Lakota Sioux, "Wakantanka, waonsila yo; Wanikiya, waonsila yo, which means, "God, have mercy on me; Jesus, have mercy on me." Suddenly I heard an inner voice, which I would later identify as the Holy Spirit, also speaking to me, "But *I have* had mercy on you through the death of my son Jesus Christ." I was stunned by this revelation because I had thought the peyote church was the ultimate means to spiritual peace and joy. But doubts had emerged in recent months that had shaken that idea. I now realized that there was no salvation through eating peyote and this so-called sacrament would not lead me to faith and eternal life.

With the conclusion of morning water and the resumption of the service, I stepped outside the church house and looked up into the clear, starlit sky. "High" on peyote and without any altar call or organ playing "Just As I Am," I thanked God for his mercy on me through Jesus' death. I also told the Lord that I would follow him no matter where that path might lead. At the meeting's conclusion I found Dindy and we began to talk. Hesitatingly, because she knew how much I liked the "peyote way," Dindy told me that she could no longer attend peyote meetings. That night had been a spiritual turning point for her as well as she realized that she could go directly to God without having to eat the bitter herb, peyote, in order to reach him. Wondering how her announcement would be received, she was overjoyed to learn that God had spoken the same thing to me during the service and that we were now spiritual twins born into the kingdom of God.

This decision brought immediate consequences. Our family had been living in cramped quarters in the church building so we needed to relocate immediately to separate ourselves from the influence of peyote. The break from our peyote friends was difficult, since our membership in the NAC was the reason we were living on the reservation. A Lakota pastor and his wife, Ted and Mamie Standing Elk, led Bible studies that we were attending, so we decided to move to Porcupine to attend the Mennonite Brethren

Church that they pastored. So we went from being the only white people in the peyote meetings to being the only non-Indians in the local Christian fellowship. Like Paul, we had to change religious communities immediately so as to progress in our new faith.

Katherine Rutt writes:

"I heard the voice of God once, which totally changed my life. I was living in a small town, and because I was not a Christian, I didn't get involved in a church. In those days the church was where you made and had friends. I found a 'perfect' house for sale in a town where I wanted to live because of friends and its social life. I persuaded my mother to pay for it since we had not sold our house. We made an offer on the property, but it was rejected so we met the owner's price. My husband went along with me, but without enthusiasm.

Meanwhile, the owner landed in the hospital and couldn't make up her mind if she really wanted to sell. I agonized over the purchase while waiting for things to work out my way. One night I was awakened by a voice, '*Do not buy that house!*' By the way, I knew it was God and not my husband. That same night he had a dream in which we had moved to the house, and one of our children was hit by a car in the road. Amazingly, I persisted for several days but finally relented and cancelled the offer. I then vowed to get involved in the town where we lived, which ultimately led to my conversion. The one road led to the country-club life, while the other led to the Christian life. I am forever grateful that I obeyed God's voice and chose the latter way."

Reflection Questions

What aspects of Paul's conversion stand out to you?

What part did Ananias play in Paul's conversion experience?

Who among your family or friends played a part in your conversion?

What experiences suggest that God was sovereignly guiding you before becoming a believer?

Have you written out an account of your conversion? Whom have you shared it with?

2

The Early Journeys

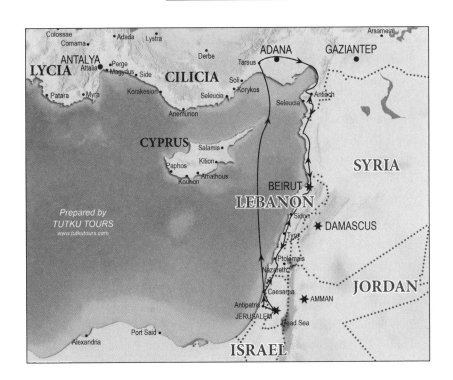

LESSON 2

God uses spiritual mentors to guide us.

²⁶ When he came to Jerusalem, he tried to join the disciples, but they were all afraid of him, not believing that he really was a disciple. ²⁷ But Barnabas took him and brought him to the apostles. Saul told them how he had seen the Lord on his journey and that the Lord had spoken to him, and how in Damascus he had preached fearlessly in the name of Jesus.[1] ²⁸ So Saul stayed with them and moved about freely in Jerusalem, speaking boldly in the name of the Lord. ²⁹ He talked and debated with the Hellenistic Jews, but they tried to kill him. ³⁰ When the believers learned of this, they took him down to Caesarea and sent him off to Tarsus. (9:26–30)

²¹ The Lord's hand was with them, and a great number of people believed and turned to the Lord. ²² News of this reached the church in Jerusalem, and they sent Barnabas to Antioch. ²³ When he arrived and saw what the grace of God had done, he was glad and encouraged them all to remain true to the Lord with all their hearts. ²⁴ He was a good man, full of the Holy Spirit and faith, and a great number of people were brought to the Lord. ²⁵ Then Barnabas went to Tarsus to look for Saul, ²⁶ and when he found him, he brought him to Antioch. So for a whole year Barnabas and Saul met with the church and taught great numbers of people. The disciples were called Christians first at Antioch. (11:21–26)

1. The text of the NIV has been changed to reflect the Greek text better: that Paul told the apostles about his own conversion, not Barnabas. See my article, "Barnabas or Saul."

Paul's Guidance

Acts provides two interesting examples of how a mentor named Barnabas helped to guide Paul in the years after his conversion. Barnabas is first introduced by his Jewish name Joseph, but the apostles called him Barnabas, which means "son of encouragement" (4:36). By birth he was a priestly Levite whose homeland was the island of Cyprus. A basilica church dedicated to Barnabas stands today near ancient Salamis, where tradition holds that he was martyred. Barnabas was a generous man who brought money to the apostles so needy believers might receive assistance (4:37).

Chapter 9 depicts a young and zealous Paul who has returned to Jerusalem for the first time after his conversion. He was eager to join the followers of Jesus, but no one trusted him. They suspected perhaps that his story was simply a trick to infiltrate the Jerusalem church and destroy it from within. So the believers were afraid to receive him into fellowship until Barnabas stepped in. He met with Paul and discovered that he was truly a changed man. Barnabas then introduced him to the apostles. During his meeting with these leaders Paul recounted the story of how Jesus had met him on the road to Damascus, forever changing his life. The result was that Paul was now accepted by the Jerusalem church and became an eloquent spokesman for the gospel.

Paul's former rage against the followers of Jesus was transformed into such a zeal for Jesus that he soon got himself in trouble. He most likely returned to the Synagogue of the Freedman to share his testimony with his former friends among the Diaspora community (6:9). These included Jews not only from Cilicia, where Tarsus was located, but also those from Ephesus in Asia, and Cyrene and Alexandria in North Africa.

However, news that Paul had become a traitor to Judaism provoked antagonism against him. His former friends now tried to kill Paul in the same way as they had killed Stephen. Realizing that Paul's life was in peril, other believers, probably advised by Barnabas, spirited Paul out of Jerusalem to Caesarea. Here they secured his passage on a ship for Tarsus, an action that undoubtedly saved Paul's life. If Paul had decided to ignore Barnabas' presumed counsel and to resist his fellow Jews, there would be no missionary journeys to speak about.

Paul's time in Tarsus is sometimes referred to as his silent years. The length of this period is unknown but certainly lasted five or more years.

Some clues suggest that Paul was active in ministry. Churches in Cilicia are mentioned twice (15:23, 41). No one except Paul is known to be in Cilicia at this time so he must have established these churches.[2] In the description of his trials Paul mentions that five times he received thirty-nine lashes from the Jews (2 Cor 11:24). This was the usual punishment that a synagogue would impose against a presumed apostate. Jewish leaders in Cilicia apparently resisted Paul's new message about Jesus and disciplined him by flogging. This was one of the trials endured by Paul that validated his apostolic ministry (2 Cor 12:12).

During his time in Tarsus a spiritual movement was beginning in nearby Antioch on the Orontes, the capital of the Roman province of Syria. Jewish believers from Cyprus and Cyrene went to Antioch and began to share the good news both with Jews and Gentiles (11:19–21). When the church in Jerusalem heard about this, the apostles sent Barnabas to disciple the new believers (11:22–24). When the work became too great for him, Barnabas remembered the zealous believer who lived in nearby Tarsus. A thought came to his mind, undoubtedly inspired by the Holy Spirit, to bring Paul to Antioch. So he made the six-day, 125 mile walk to find Paul. Luke's use of the Greek word *anazēteō*[3] ("look for"; 11:25) suggests that Barnabas had to do a bit of searching to locate him.

Paul had been witnessing about Jesus around Tarsus, and now his faithfulness was rewarded: a new door was opening to him. His years in Cilicia had served to deepen his faith and mature him in ministry. Given his zeal, he was undoubtedly eager to launch out further. He returned to Antioch with Barnabas and ministered under his tutelage for a year. The order of their names, Barnabas and Saul, suggests that the former took the lead.

The fruit of their teamwork was remarkable: great numbers were saved and grew in the Lord. These new converts made such a visible impact that outsiders began to call them *Christianoi*—"followers of Christ." Their partnership continued, and as we will see, Barnabas' role as a mentor would be a key to Paul's future ministry success.

---

2. For the probable locations of these churches see my article, "Cilicia."

3. For example, Luke also uses the word twice in his Gospel (Luke 2:44–45) to describe the efforts of Mary and Joseph to locate Jesus among their friends and relatives as well as in Jerusalem.

God uses spiritual mentors to guide us.

Guidance Today

My encounter on a stairwell landing in the Divinity School building was unplanned. J. Rodman Williams was my professor at Regent University, and as a noted theologian in the renewal movement, he was one of the reasons I had enrolled in its Master's degree program. Matter-of-factly, Dr. Williams asked whether I would be interested in serving as his graduate assistant. Initially taken aback but pleased with the offer, I told him that I would talk to my wife and pray about it. That meeting was to begin a working relationship and friendship with Dr. Williams that continued for over two decades until his death in 2008. Initially I began to grade student papers and help organize his class notes. Dr. Williams, later Rod when I became his peer, saw in me the potential to become a scholar and professor. Rod hoped that I would follow in his steps as a theologian, but my interest instead was in New Testament studies, especially the book of Revelation.

My responsibilities serving Dr. Williams soon broadened. He had begun to write his three-volume magnum opus, *Renewal Theology*, and had signed a contract to publish it. One day he asked me if I would serve as his initial editor for the books. Still a student, I was a bit intimidated to suggest corrections or additions, but with his characteristic humility Rod told me that he welcomed and valued my comments. This editorial work prepared me for the writing and editing that I still do today.

In 1989 an opportunity opened at the Christian Broadcasting Network for me to become first a writer for and later general editor of a discipleship curriculum called *Living By The Book*. Rod had three courses in its twenty-course curriculum. The project introduced me to the publishing side of scholarship. In 1994 I edited a *Festschrift* for Rod called *Spirit and Renewal* that honored him on his seventy-fifth birthday. This dedicatory volume was my first book project, and in it I also published my first essay.[4]

During the days when Dindy and I were students at Regent, we were also raising our four children. So we had little extra money. But the editorial work that I did for Rod and also for his wife Jo, who herself is a novelist, helped to pay the tuition fees for Dindy's Master's program and later for the tuition for doctoral study at the University of South Africa. So this collaboration brought great financial blessing to us as well. Most of all, Rod gave wise counsel regarding scholarship and ministry. He was especially encouraging while I was writing my doctoral thesis, a mountain that seemed

4. Wilson, "Revelation 19.10."

insurmountable at times. Looking back, I am full of gratitude that God sent such a godly, influential mentor into my life.

James Bultema writes:

"When my wife Renata and I first traveled to Turkey in the fall of 1990, we had a simple but clear vision in mind: to start churches where no churches exist. An underlying assumption was that those churches would be dis-tinctly *Turkish* churches. Therefore, soon after our arrival, we began the arduous process of learning theuTkish language and culture.

Simultaneous to my finishing two years of full-time language study, I received a completely unforeseen request: to serve as the interim pastor of the historic English-speaking Union Church of Istanbul, where we would worship on Sundays. The request seemed as remote as Las Vegas to my personal vision for ministry in Turkey. However, when I shared the request with my sagacious mentor back in our home church, he said, 'I suggest that you accept the request. Whether or not it is ultimately from the Lord will become clear.'

I have never been able to describe adequately the elation in my heart as I preached my first sermon as the interim pastor of the Union Church. In fact, that whole year for me was growth-filled and gratifying. But I was somewhat torn within. I loved international-church ministry, but longed as well to start a new church, in line with our original sense of purpose.

Toward the end of that interim year, Renata and I defined four vi-able options for our future ministry. All were attractive opportunities to us, but over time we were able to reason two options out of consideration, because they would have involved pastoring established churches rather than starting new ones. However, we agonized over a decision between the final two options. Worse yet, Renata strongly preferred one option (staying in Istanbul and starting a new international church to the north along the European side of the Bosporus Strait), and I preferred the other (moving to Antalya and starting an international church there).

We tentatively moved ahead with testing the waters of both options, knowing as we did that one option would eventually lose out to the other. Groups of hopeful people in both cities were doing their best to persuade us to join them, knowing as they did that God's will in the matter may in fact differ from theirs. A distinction, however, was that the group in Istanbul were close friends, and the group in Antalya were largely unknown to us.

This mattered greatly to Renata, who would shed tears at the thought of leaving behind her revitalizing friendships in Istanbul. I must add that our two children were the same way.

As the labor of our deliberation intensified and a final decision had to be born, God's guidance finally came. But it arrived as mysteriously as it did momentously. Afterwards I would tell people that the decision arrived like an owl in the night: none of us family members heard or saw the feathered decision arrive, but suddenly there it was, palpable, and we all heard the wisdom of its song. Preparations to move to Antalya were begun.

Upon reflection, I can say this about that mysterious arrival of God's will so long ago: it came as vision for that particular option grew. Other UCI leaders and I formed a plan whereby the new church in Antalya could be established as a UCI church plant. Co-workers in the Union Church joined Renata and me in offering, in a prominent hotel in Antalya, an experimental Easter worship service in 1996, and an encouraging number of locals attended. Renata and our children began to envisage friendships taking shape with new acquaintances in Antalya. "Where there is no vision, the people perish" is oft-quoted from Proverbs 29:18a (KJV). Similarly, I believe that our Antalya option would have perished, at the outset, had we not nurtured within our minds and hearts an inspiring sense of vision for satisfying new friendships and fulfilling ministry."

Reflection Questions

What were some characteristics of Barnabas that made him an ideal mentor for Paul?

What did Barnabas do to encourage Paul's faith and ministry?

Name someone in your life who has served as a mentor to you.

What character qualities of your mentor do you remember?

How did this mentor encourage you in Christian life and ministry?

Lesson 3

God uses prophets to guide us.

[27] During this time some prophets came down from Jerusalem to Antioch. [28] One of them, named Agabus, stood up and through the Spirit predicted that a severe famine would spread over the entire Roman world. (This happened during the reign of Claudius.) [29] The disciples, as each one was able, decided to provide help for the brothers and sisters living in Judea. [30] This they did, sending their gift to the elders by Barnabas and Saul. (11:27–30)

Paul's Guidance

For the first time in Acts the Holy Spirit speaks a prophetic word that will give direction to Paul. The occasion appears to be a gathering of believers in Antioch for worship. A group of prophets recognized by the Jerusalem church had traveled some 370 miles north to Antioch, a journey of around twenty days. While they were encouraging the believers there, a prophet named Agabus arose and predicted through the Spirit that a severe famine would occur in the future. Luke provides an approximate time for this event—the reign of Claudius (AD 41–54). However, the Jewish historian Josephus is more specific: it occurred between AD 44–48 (*A.J.* 20.101).

Agabus' prophecy encouraged the believers in Antioch to respond with a generous gift, according to each one's financial means. The offering was for Jewish brothers and sisters in Judea whom they did not know. This is the fourth occasion in Acts where generosity is demonstrated by the early believers. Previously they had shared possessions (4:32–37), distributed food to widows (6:1), and helped the poor through good deeds (9:36–39). Luke demonstrates his concern for the needy by showing repeatedly that benevolence characterizes believers guided by the Holy Spirit and is an important tool for spreading the gospel.

Barnabas and Saul were chosen to take the offering to Jerusalem, undoubtedly accompanied by the prophets who were returning home. Titus traveled with them as well (Gal 2:1). This was now Paul's second visit to Jerusalem after his conversion.[1] These representatives from Antioch delivered the offering to the apostles. Had they known about Agabus' prophecy of a coming famine before that? Probably not, since the Spirit apparently first revealed this in Antioch.

The believers in Jerusalem and Judea must have responded with concern upon hearing about the predicted famine. Nevertheless, they must also have been encouraged that the Holy Spirit was preparing them to face the difficult days ahead. The disapproval that some felt towards the Gentile believers must have faded as they accepted their generous offering. This tangible expression of love undoubtedly served to break down cultural and social divisions between the Jewish and Gentile believers, which sometimes manifested themselves. Perhaps this partly explains why Titus was not required to be circumcised (Gal 2:3).

Since Paul was in Jerusalem, he was able to tell the apostles the gospel message he was proclaiming to the Gentiles (Gal 2:2). They must have quizzed him about his ministry activity in Cilicia after they had sent him home to Tarsus (9:30). Paul undoubtedly shared about the churches that he planted there, and with Barnabas described the growth of the church in Antioch among both Jews and Gentiles. In contrast to the zealous and headstrong young man who had arrived from Arabia years earlier, the apostles now saw a mature, seasoned servant of the Lord. Upon the conclusion of their mission of relief, Barnabas and Paul returned to Antioch accompanied by John Mark, the cousin of Barnabas (12:25; see Col 4:10). The success of this journey, motivated by Agabus' prophecy, undoubtedly gave Paul confidence in the Spirit's ability to guide his life, something he would learn more about on future journeys.

---

1. How Paul's early journeys in Acts intersect with Paul's own description of his journeys to Jerusalem in Galatians chapters 1–2 remains a debated topic among scholars. My perspective accords with that of my friend Ben Witherington who discusses the issue in his commentary *Acts*, 90–97.

Guidance Today

Dick Eastman, the international president of Every Home for Christ, was preaching at Kempsville Presbyterian Church (KPC) on April 13, 1986. After the first of our two services that Sunday, Dick was praying and the Lord spoke to him to prophesy to our congregation. Through Dick, the Holy Spirit challenged KPC to become a Fountainhead church that would become a stream of spiritual life both at home and to the nations. His prophecy was grounded in Scripture, as is all genuine prophecy. He quoted Isaiah 58:11: "The Lord will guide you always; he will satisfy your needs in a sun-scorched land and will strengthen your frame. You will be like a well-watered garden, like a spring whose waters never fail" (see Appendix 4 for the complete prophecy).

I was out of town that day, but Dindy recalls the occasion clearly: "It was a powerful moment, and many of us did not want to leave the sanctuary even after the service ended. The pastor invited us to linger as long as we liked, so several of us remained to pray. I had been asking God if it was his will that I pursue a Master's degree at Regent University, and this seemed like the perfect atmosphere in which God might speak to me and make his will clear. I was kneeling at a pew facing one of the double doors leading into the sanctuary. After a time of seeking God, I suddenly had a clear 'picture' of those double doors swinging open towards me. I then had the distinct impression that God was going to 'open' a way for me to attend school! In fact, not long afterwards, he did!"

Our pastor at the time, Don Rossire, as well as the session (the elders in a Presbyterian church) began to embrace the prophecy. Our pastor of international ministries, Andy Jackson, particularly championed this vision until his departure in 1996. After Don left in 1989, David Gyertson and Dick Little served as interim pastors. Spiritual momentum, stimulated by the prophecy, continued to grow. Dindy joined the KPC staff in 1989 and recalls the ongoing influence of the Fountainhead prophecy. In 1992 Chuck Wickman was called as pastor, and under his leadership the church continued to blossom through the inspiration of the Fountainhead vision.

Fruit from the prophecy was evidenced in various ways. Eight men came under pastoral care of the session as they prepared for ordination in ministry. Over a dozen individuals and couples were sent and supported in overseas ministry. The building became inadequate to handle congregational growth, so "Fountainhead" was adopted as the theme in KPC's capital campaign to raise money for its expansion. KPC began to mobilize its members to do prayer walking overseas in the 10/40 Window, to host local seminars for Perspectives on the World Christian Movement, and to expand its local food and clothing ministry that reached many needy people.

In 1992 Dick Eastman returned to KPC to conduct one of his Change the World School of Prayer seminars. This time I was there as Dick recounted his initial delivery of the Fountainhead prophecy given six years before. After his message Dindy and I were among those who went forward for prayer. Our pastor Andy Jackson asked Dick if he had a prophetic word for those gathered on the platform. Dick quoted Revelation 3:7–8 in response, declaring that God had opened a door before us that no one could shut and that we should go forth as ambassadors to the nations. My first visit to Turkey followed shortly thereafter.

Later the media director Orlen Stauffer prepared both a Fountainhead image and a logo that hung in the sanctuary. Reproduced weekly on the cover of the bulletin, it reminded the congregation of its prophetic calling. Dick Eastman had spoken as a prophet that Sunday morning, and the effect of his inspired speech changed the direction of our congregation—Dindy and me included.

Reflection Questions

Why do you think the believers in Antioch accepted the prophecy of Agabus?

How did the church respond to his prophecy?

In what ways might the generous offering have changed the perception of Jewish believers towards their Gentile counterparts?

Has your church ever received something like a Fountainhead Prophecy?

If so, what has been the spiritual fruit from that prophecy?

3

The First Journey

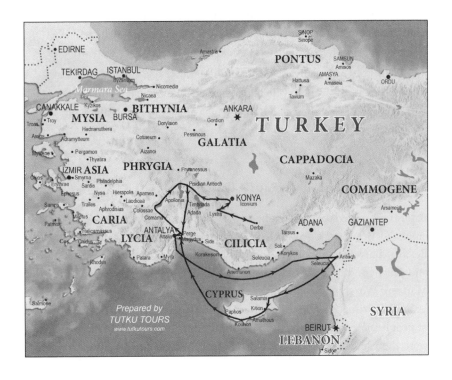

Prepared by
TUTKU TOURS
www.tutkutours.com

Lesson 4

God uses church leaders to guide us.

¹ Now in the church at Antioch there were prophets and teachers: Barnabas, Simeon called Niger, Lucius of Cyrene, Manaen (who had been brought up with Herod the tetrarch) and Saul. ² While they were worshiping the Lord and fasting, the Holy Spirit said, "Set apart for me Barnabas and Saul for the work to which I have called them." ³ So after they had fasted and prayed, they placed their hands on them and sent them off. (13:1–3)

Paul's Guidance

After their return to Antioch, Barnabas and Paul continued to teach the disciples. As the church grew, a leadership team emerged to care for its needs. Besides Barnabas and Paul, three other men are mentioned as prophets and teachers in the church: Simeon called Niger, Lucius of Cyrene, and Manaen. Worship and fasting were spiritual disciplines practiced by these leaders. During one of their gatherings, the Holy Spirit spoke another word of prophecy seemingly through one of these three men. Barnabas and Paul were then set apart for a new work to which they had already been called. The Holy Spirit had apparently been stirring their hearts to leave Antioch and preach to Jews and Gentiles who had not heard the gospel. All they were waiting for was direction to depart.

Paul and Barnabas were learning an important principle about guidance: a delay may occur between sensing God's leading to do something and the actual time to implement that direction. In their case we don't know how long the time-lag was. But the moment had finally arrived for Barnabas and Paul to be consecrated by the other leaders for the work ahead. Perhaps the purpose of this particular meeting was to seek God about *when* that should happen, and the Holy Spirit indicated that *now* was the time. Hands were now laid on the two men, probably at a gathering of the entire community, and they along with John Mark were sent on their way.

Verse 4 states that they were also "sent on their way by the Holy Spirit." So the apostolic party received both a human and a divine send off. Because of the formative role that the church in Antioch played in Paul's spiritual development, he maintained a connection to the church there throughout his ministry. At the conclusion of each of his first two journeys, Paul returned to Antioch to report what God had done. There is no record either in Acts or in Paul's letters that the believers in Antioch supported him financially. But this church must surely have served as a base of prayer support and encouragement for all his ministry activity. It is easy to focus on Paul's preaching gifts and supernatural ministry as reasons for his success in church planting. However, the support of the leaders and the prayers of the saints in churches like Antioch, Philippi, and Ephesus were also key factors in his spiritual success.

Guidance Today

Soon after arriving in Antalya in 2011, our pastor James Bultema asked us whether we wanted to join the St. Paul Union Church (SPUC). He affirmed that we could hold joint membership with our home church back in the U.S. Dindy and I eagerly accepted, and at the next business meeting we were received into membership.

A puzzling thing to me is that some Christians today do not feel a need to join a local church. I know that some have been "burned" by pastors who created a negative spiritual environment. Others have had disappointing experiences with "hypocrites" in the congregation. Or perhaps they have been hurt by something that an elder or deacon said or did. Nevertheless, the proper response is not to withdraw from fellowship but to receive counseling, healing, and then find a healthy congregation of followers of Christ.

Ever since our conversion, in all our moves around the world, we have prayed that the Lord would lead us to the right local church. Usually we have benefited from the spiritual leaders over us. However, there have been exceptions. The toxic leadership style of one pastor stretched our faith and patience to the limit. And we also attended churches where two congregations were negatively impacted by the pastor's adultery and one congregation by the pastor's financial mismanagement.

As we have sought the Lord for guidance, especially over major decisions, part of that process has been to consult pastors, elders, and small group leaders for their input and wisdom. While praying about where to attend graduate school, Phil Joseph, the school president in Mobridge, South Dakota, provided key counsel on the matter. Occasionally we have not followed such counsel. For example, one pastor discouraged me from seeking formal academic training in the Bible. Later our pastor friend Don White did encourage me to attend Bible school. So we always weigh the counsel of spiritual leaders carefully in our decision making.

Since 1984 we have been members of Kempsville Presbyterian Church in Virginia Beach, Virginia. KPC remains our home church, and the congregation continues to support us prayerfully and financially. Each fall when we return to the U.S., we meet with the pastor—now Steve Keller— and give him a report about what has been happening with us over the past year. We feel this accountability factor has been part of our success in living overseas for over a decade.

Here in Antalya we continue as members of SPUC, planted by James and his wife Renata and now pastored by Dennis Massaro. For years James had encouraged us to move to Antalya and become part of the church here. Eventually God's timing allowed that relocation to occur in 2011 after our season of ministry in Istanbul was over. At SPUC we enthusiastically participate in all its activities—praying, teaching, ushering, or preaching whenever we're called upon. Dindy serves on the church council as well. Because of its holiday environment, Antalya hosts numerous people on vacation or seeking spiritual R & R. It has been gratifying to see many of them receive guidance regarding the next stage of life and ministry as our congregation has prayed for them.

Anna Griffith writes:

"Since being baptized at nine years of age, I've had this insatiable desire to study Scripture. When my husband's job brought us close to Abilene, Texas, I started taking courses towards a Masters in Biblical Studies at Abilene Christian University. One pivotal day in the early 1990s, I dropped into Dr. Tony Ash's office to straighten out my transcript.

He asked, 'Do you know how close you are to a Masters of Divinity?' I learned that I lacked only thirty hours in the ninety-hour program. I replied, 'Tony, what would a middle-aged American housewife in the Churches of Christ do with a M. Div?' (At that point in the CoC women were not allowed to minister and get paid.) With aggravation, Tony shot back, 'Why don't you let the Lord decide that?' Dumbfounded, I mumbled that I'd think about it.

While backing out of his office, I literally collided with Dr. Charles Siburt, head of the Doctor of Ministry program at ACU. He exclaimed, 'Anna Griffith! When are you going to get into the D. Min. program?' 'Dr. Siburt, I don't even have a M. Div. yet.' 'Well, *Get It!*' he responded and just walked away. I went back to my car, thinking that these two academic giants in the Church of Christ had lost every marble they ever had. No woman had ever been admitted to either the M. Div. or D. Min programs at ACU. And even if she graduated, how would she ever have a career in the CoC? By that time I was in my early 50s so I just shook my head.

Two weeks later we learned that our youngest son was HIV positive. I was devastated and begged him, '*Run*, don't walk, to God.' He replied, 'Mom, the church isn't doing anything about AIDS.' He was right. Early in the 1990s, no one was talking about it or addressing it. And I thought, 'Over my dead body!' and then said to God, 'I don't want to work in AIDS ministry.' He smiled back and said, 'Fine, but you're it so go!'

I applied to ACU and was accepted for the M. Div. program. By the time I graduated, everyone knew I'd work in AIDS ministry. The higher-ups knew that none of the men wanted to go there, but they wanted someone to do a good job in the AIDS ministry. Before I graduated with the M. Div., I was accepted into the D. Min. program, the first woman at ACU to do either. By 1998 Africa was desperate for help. Short story: I've been to Africa nine times to help small churches deal with their AIDS problems—educating, counseling, and preaching. It was all God!"

Ed Vinieratos writes:

"After the 1986 catastrophic space shuttle disaster that led to my job loss, multi-year unemployment, and marital separation plus the death of my mother, I left California in late 1992. In Oregon I was also unsuccessful in my job search. As I was rather depressed because of all the closed doors, a pastor counseled me to be all that I could be in His name.

At church the next Sunday while singing a Christmas carol, God spoke in a commanding though not audible voice that still was louder than the music and vocals filling the church. He spoke, 'Go to Russia!' I was astonished and asked, 'Russia?' I was a Cold War veteran and retired USAF Reserve officer. How? Where? When? These were questions that I kept asking after the service.

Over the next several days God revealed the answers to my quest. I remembered my seminary training completed ten years prior: missions would be my purpose. I was to return to my alma mater, Fuller Seminary in Pasadena, and its School of World Missions for guidance on the how. A door opened in St. Petersburg in May 1993, and I began my twenty-three year odyssey of service there that ended in August 2016."

Reflection Questions

What were the leaders doing when guidance for Paul and Barnabas was received?

What was the Holy Spirit's role in their calling?

Have you ever fasted while praying about a decision? If so, what was the result?

Name some leaders you have counseled with while seeking guidance.

In what ways did that pastor or leader help with your decision making?

Lesson 5

God uses human networks to guide us.

[4] The two of them, sent on their way by the Holy Spirit, went down to Seleucia and sailed from there to Cyprus. [5] When they arrived at Salamis, they proclaimed the word of God in the Jewish synagogues. John was with them as their helper. [6] They traveled through the whole island until they came to Paphos. (13:4–6a)

Paul's Guidance

Now that the Holy Spirit had released Barnabas and Paul for ministry, where were they to go? The Euphrates River located east of Antioch was the eastern boundary of the Roman Empire so that direction was problematic. Paul had already planted churches in Cilicia to the northwest, so it was unnecessary to preach there again. Major cities south toward Jerusalem had already been evangelized by others.

Earlier Luke had mentioned that Barnabas came from Cyprus (4:26). Cyprus is the third largest island in the Mediterranean Sea and located within sight of the eastern Mediterranean coast. Local tradition places his home at Salamis, a major harbor city and former capital of the island. Since Barnabas already had an existing network within the Jewish community in Salamis, the apostles decided to minister first in the synagogues there.[1]

---

1. Marshall affirms that guidance has human and divine components. After noting that Barnabas had family ties on Cyprus, he writes, "From a human point of view, therefore, it was natural for the mission to start there, but the missionaries felt guided by the Spirit to do so" (*Acts*, 216).

John Mark served as their apprentice helper, and the three of them made the sixteen-mile walk from Antioch down to its port, Seleucia Pieria. There they found passage on a ship sailing to Salamis on Cyprus' northeastern coast. Depending on wind conditions, the voyage would have taken only a few days.

Although Luke does not mention any converts in Salamis, such an argument from silence does not rule out spiritual success. Generally in Acts when the word of God is preached, people believe in Jesus Christ (4:2; 17:3, 13, 23). Luke, for the sake of brevity, occasionally does not record the spiritual results at a city, assuming that his readers understand that some listeners always believed. Leaving Salamis, the apostles journeyed along the southern coast of Cyprus along the Roman road connecting its cities. Some had Jewish communities for centuries, such as Kition (Larnaca). The island's Hebrew name Kittim probably derives from the name of this city (Jer 2:10). Along the way they probably spoke in the synagogues of other cities such as Amathus and Kourion.[2] Beginning their journey in a place where Barnabas was already networked proved to be key to the apostles' success on the island. This mirrored Paul's success in Cilicia where he similarly had a natural network, since he had grown up in Tarsus.

Guidance Today

In 1987 I completed a Masters of Arts in Biblical Studies at Regent University. Realizing that teaching and writing was my ultimate calling, I knew that a doctorate in biblical studies was necessary. The only programs nearby were at the University of Virginia and Union Theological Seminary, neither of which were possible. So I began to look overseas. My friend Jim Funari had been accepted for doctoral study at the University of Aberdeen. He and his wife Susan had most of their assets invested in a house at the time and couldn't complete its sale in a timely fashion. So they didn't have the resources to move with their three children to Scotland and study full-time. If Jim had found the costs too prohibitive, I realized that the U.K. was not an option for me either. Our family had relocated so many times in pursuit of education and ministry that Dindy and I had decided that another move would be too disruptive. At the time our daughter Leilani was attending Virginia Commonwealth University; Winema was in a private Christian high school, Jim in junior high, and David in middle school. So I began

2. For further details see my article, "Syria, Cilicia, and Cyprus," 498–99.

to ask God to show me an alternative, but became discouraged when no educational door seemed to be opening.

In 1991 the Society for Pentecostal Studies held its annual meeting at Regent University. After a session I met a South African scholar named Henry Lederle, who was then teaching at the University of South Africa. (Later we were to become colleagues at Oral Roberts University.) I asked Henry whether he could recommend any doctoral programs in New Testament in South Africa. He immediately mentioned his own university—Unisa. Then Henry told me something amazing: the university was distance-based, and I could remain in Virginia throughout my doctoral program! Unisa follows the British system so I only needed to write a thesis. I applied to its doctoral program in New Testament and was accepted. (Unisa did subsequently require me to complete a one-year course in Classical and Patristic Greek and Greco-Roman history before matriculating, which was the hardest course that I've ever taken.) In 1996 I submitted the thesis, and in May 1997 Dindy and I traveled to Pretoria for my graduation ceremony where I was awarded the degree of Doctor of Literature and Philosophy (D. Litt. et Phil.).

This South African connection has proved fortuitous for subsequent scholarly activities. I later received academic appointments with the University of South Africa and Stellenbosch University. Many of my articles have been published in South African journals. Since 1994 I have been a member of the New Testament Society of Southern Africa and have developed productive relationships with colleagues there. Traveling to South Africa periodically for conferences has been one of the joys of my life.

In March 1997 I was in Oakland, California, attending another meeting of the Society for Pentecostal Studies. There I met James Shelton, who was teaching New Testament at Oral Roberts University. During a conversation I mentioned the completion of my doctorate, and Jim in turn told me that a teaching position in New Testament would be available in the undergraduate theology department that fall. He encouraged me to apply for the position. Before starting my doctoral studies some professors had suggested that I *not* major in New Testament because there would be few teaching jobs available. But because I wanted to research and write on Revelation, my degree had to be in New Testament. I applied for the ORU job, traveled there for an interview, and was hired. God did provide a job in my chosen area, and I became a colleague of Jim.

Networking with Henry Lederle and James Shelton at these annual meetings of the Society for Pentecostal Studies changed my professional life. My subsequent teaching positions, research appointments, and book and article publications would not have been possible without a doctoral degree. The teaching opportunity at ORU, albeit later in life at age 47, initiated my academic teaching career. God amazingly made a way for all this to happen while at the same time meeting the needs of our family.

Dindy Wilson writes:

"After our move to Virginia Beach in 1984, I began to work at the Christian Broadcasting Network (CBN). My supervisor there was Martha Bennett, and a longstanding friendship with her developed. Years later Martha's husband Stuart, who is a filmmaker, contacted us about making films in Turkey about biblical subjects. In 2014 Stuart and Martha traveled to Turkey to make features with Mark and our friend Andy Jackson on the city of Ephesus and in 2015 with Mark on the life of St. Nicholas.

One of my coworkers at CBN was Jill Thompson, and she and I also became good friends. When I attended Regent University, Jill was a classmate, and after graduation we worked together at Kempsville Presbyterian Church. Jill kept telling me about her sister Julie Zylstra who lived in Seattle and that we should meet her when we visited our family there. A year after moving to Turkey, Mark and I finally met Julie and her husband Russ. They kindly offered to host a gathering of their friends at their lovely home, a visit that has become an annual tradition. Each fall when we visit our family, we also share with the Zylstras and their circle what we've been doing in Turkey during that year. These are just two examples of how networking through my job at CBN blossomed into relationships that have continued for decades."

Reflection Questions

Why was Cyprus chosen as the first place the apostles went on their mission?

Where had Paul begun his own church-planting ministry, and why did he have a network there?

Identify some of the networks with which you are linked?

Can you share how the Holy Spirit has used a network to give you guidance?

LESSON 6

God uses providential encounters to guide us.

[6] They came to Paphos. There they met a Jewish sorcerer and false prophet named Bar-Jesus, [7] who was an attendant of the proconsul, Sergius Paulus. The proconsul, an intelligent man, sent for Barnabas and Saul because he wanted to hear the word of God. [8] But Elymas the sorcerer (for that is what his name means) opposed them and tried to turn the proconsul from the faith. [9] Then Saul, who was also called Paul, filled with the Holy Spirit, looked straight at Elymas and said, [10] "You are a child of the devil and an enemy of everything that is right! You are full of all kinds of deceit and trickery. Will you never stop perverting the right ways of the Lord? [11] Now the hand of the Lord is against you. You are going to be blind for a time, not even able to see the light of the sun." Immediately mist and darkness came over him, and he groped about, seeking someone to lead him by the hand. [12] When the proconsul saw what had happened, he believed, for he was amazed at the teaching about the Lord. [13] From Paphos, Paul and his companions sailed to Perga in Pamphylia, where John left them to return to Jerusalem. [14] From Perga they went on to Pisidian Antioch. (13:6b–14)

Paul's Guidance

After traveling along the southern coast of Cyprus, the apostolic party arrived in Paphos. In the late fourth century BC the Ptolemies moved the capital from Salamis to their new city Nea Paphos on the island's southwestern tip. For almost three centuries the city was oriented southward toward Alexandria, Egypt, the Ptolemaic capital. In 58 BC the Romans annexed the island, and Paphos served as their capital as well.

As they preached the gospel in Paphos, Paul and Barnabas encountered a Jewish sorcerer named Elymas. He was the spiritual adviser to the Roman proconsul named Sergius Paulus. The governor invited the apostles to his administrative center to share their message with him. This same palace with its beautiful mosaic floors has been excavated by archaeologists. Elymas tried to dissuade his educated patron that the message of the apostles was not true. Paul responded with a strong invective exposing the source of Elymas's opposition—the devil. When Elymas was struck with blindness, Sergius Paulus realized the power of the gospel and believed.

The nature and extent of his faith has been questioned, for there is no record of him being baptized or receiving the Holy Spirit. Yet verse 12 states clearly that he "believed," the same verb *pisteuō* used over thirty times in Acts to indicate faith in the Lord Jesus. From Luke's perspective the governor's faith was the same as that of Lydia (16:15) or the Philippian jailer (16:34).

From Paphos the three sailed directly north to Asia Minor (Turkey), arriving in Pamphylia at Perga's seaport of Magydus. They then walked approximately nine miles to Perga along a road, which has a well-preserved portion still visible east of Antalya's airport. A Roman historian, Stephen Mitchell, has suggested that Paul's encounter with Sergius Paulus was the reason that the apostles turned northward to Pisidian Antioch.[1] There are several unstated reasons that support this suggestion. The first is geographical. Prevailing winds and currents in the Mediterranean favored sailing from Paphos to Judea or North Africa, not Asia Minor. Travelers to Pamphylia generally departed Cyprus from the northern coast, not from Paphos, suggesting that the turn northward was unplanned.

A second reason is archaeological. Latin inscriptions discovered in Pisidian Antioch name L. Sergius Paullus *filio*, the son of the proconsul, and his daughter Sergia Paulla who was married to C. Caristanius Fronto, whose family was also prominent in Antioch. So Sergius Paulus was a Roman landowner and senator from Pisidian Antioch, whose family had colonized the city in 25 BC.

---

1. Mitchell's hypothesis and other related issues are discussed in my article, "Saint Paul in Pamphylia."

A third reason is textual: John Mark left Barnabas and Paul at Perga, a seemingly strange decision that would have future repercussions (15:37–39). Various reasons have been suggested for his desertion (see Lesson 9), but the most persuasive is that he had not joined Barnabas and Paul to evangelize Asia Minor, but rather Alexandria and Cyrene. He was interested in preaching to the large Jewish community there. North African Jews were active in the Synagogue of the Freedman in Jerusalem where Paul attended (6:9). Jewish believers from Cyprus and Cyrene first preached the gospel to the Gentiles in Antioch (11:20). And one of the leaders at Antioch was Lucius of Cyrene (13:1). Later church traditions identify John Mark as the founder of the North African church, so he apparently preached there later, perhaps after he and Barnabas left Cyprus on their second visit (15:39).[2]

A fourth clue is given by Luke: Paul and Barnabas do not stop and preach the gospel in Perga. Instead they head directly to Pisidian Antioch, another indication that this is their destination. Only on their return do they preach in Perga (14:25). It is likely that Sergius Paulus provided letters of introduction to the leaders of the Roman colony in Pisidian Antioch. The governor also might have provided transport on a Roman vessel from Paphos. (It would be difficult for John Mark to desert at Paphos and refuse the governor's hospitality.) From Perga the imperial highway—the Via Sebaste—ran to Pisidian Antioch, the head of the road (*caput viae*).

All of this circumstantial evidence points to something significant occurring after Sergius Paulus came to faith. Paul apparently interpreted his offer to commend them to the Roman officials in Pisidian Antioch as a providential sign that they were to change the journey's direction. The result was that four churches were planted in the province of Galatia—Pisidian Antioch, Iconium, Lystra, and Derbe. Perga probably became the site of another church after Paul preached there (14:25). In my view these were the churches that Paul later addressed in his letter to the Galatians.

One final observation: from now on Luke no longer uses the Jewish name Saul but instead the Roman name Paul (13:9). It has been suggested that Paul changed his name in Paphos from Saul to Paul after meeting his namesake there. But this is not possible since Paul was born a Roman citizen (22:28). All Roman citizens had three names: praenomen, nomen, and cognomen (personal, family, and family branch). Unfortunately, only his cognomen is known—Paul.

---

2. This connection with North Africa is discussed further in Davis and Wilson, "Destination."

Guidance Today

After graduating from Trinity Bible College in 1982, our family moved to Mobridge, SD, where I taught at the Central Indian Bible College for two years. I began to take some seminary classes at this time through the Assemblies of God Theological Seminary, the then North American Baptist (now Sioux Falls) Seminary, and Wheaton Graduate School. Because the door to ministry with the Assemblies of God was closed (see Lesson 10), we began to look for other options, particularly where to continue graduate studies. My sister Marla and her family were living in Thousand Oaks, California, so we decided to take an exploratory trip west to see if a school on the West Coast might be an option.

So in 1983 our family piled into a well-used Chrysler New Yorker given to us by my father, and feeling a bit like the Beverly Hillbillies, we headed to California. I enrolled in a two-week intensive course on the patristic fathers at Fuller Theological Seminary. But as we investigated the cost of living in the L.A. area, we realized it would be too expensive to raise a family while attending graduate school there. We also considered California Theological Seminary in Fresno, where one of my undergraduate professors was then teaching. But as we prayed about Fresno, we felt no leading to check out the school. This proved to be a good decision because the seminary closed a few years later.

Back in South Dakota I began reading about a new graduate program in biblical studies at CBN (now Regent) University. Since I had never wanted to live on the East Coast, it was with great reluctance that I boarded a train to Washington, D.C. There I borrowed a car from my Aunt Eloise and drove down to Virginia Beach. Soon after my arrival on Regent's beautiful, colonial-style campus, the Holy Spirit spoke inaudibly to my spirit that this was where I was to attend seminary.

I called Dindy and shared this word of direction, and we decided that I should look into possible home rentals. I contacted a realtor and arranged to look at a house near the university. While viewing the house, I met the neighbors, Bob and Janyce O'Brien, and discovered that they were believers. Their friendliness and hospitality touched me. I learned that the house would be available for rent in August, the exact time we would need to move in. Later I called Dindy and told her both about the house and that I had already met the neighbors. We agreed that the Lord wanted us to rent this house, so the next day I signed a contract with the realtor and returned to South Dakota to prepare for our relocation.

This providential encounter has proved significant until today. Bob and Janyce introduced us to their church, Kempsville Presbyterian, which we soon started to attend too. Bob taught a course at KPC on Christian stewardship that transformed our approach to finances. We slowly became debt-free, which later gave us the financial freedom to move to Turkey. Bob later became our financial planner, a role he's still in today. This all happened through a providential encounter when a realtor brought me to a house on Janet Court to check out as a possible rental.

"Tutku Tours" read the banner above a display booth in the exhibition hall of the Convention Center in San Antonio. In 2004 I was in Texas to attend the annual meeting of the Society of Biblical Literature. I began to read some of brochures on the table that were advertising biblical tours to Turkey. At the time I had been living in Izmir for just six months and was somewhat of a novice at leading biblical tours in Turkey. So I introduced myself to Levent Oral, the owner of the Turkish agency also located in Izmir. We had a long conversation, and I told Levent about my scholarly interests in Turkey's Jewish and Christian history. He described his own vision of bringing professors, students, pastors, and church groups to Turkey to experience its many biblical sites. Discovering such common interests immediately bonded us. I took some of his literature and promised to visit him after my return to Izmir. That visit took place, and a productive collaboration and enduring friendship with Levent was born. Since then I have been leading tours for Tutku Tours to biblical sites both in Turkey and in other Mediterranean countries.

In 2007 I was showing Hershel Shanks, editor of *Biblical Archaeology Review*, and his colleague Suzanne Singer around several sites in western Turkey. At Priene we met with the director of the German archaeological excavation. Hershel asked him why the synagogue there had never been excavated, and the lack of financial resources was cited as the reason. Hershel's offer to sponsor the excavation was accepted, and I was tasked with representing BAS during the synagogue's excavation, something I did with Nadin Burkhardt from 2009–2011.[3] While in Izmir on this trip, the three of us met Levent at a favorite waterfront restaurant—Mezzaluna. After dinner, Levent remembers Hershel telling him, "Levent, you and I will have a good relationship." At the time they were not collaborating on any tours or projects. Hershel's words were almost prophetic because shortly after Tutku

---

3. For the report of our interesting findings, see Burkhardt and Wilson, "Late Antique Synagogue."

began to produce tours for the Biblical Archaeology Society. And I was also thrust into the middle of developing and conducting BAS biblical tours for Tutku. A providential encounter with Levent in San Antonio was the beginning of our personal friendship and business relationship that continues until today.

Dan Gutierrez writes:

"One day I was bored and decided to go to a go-kart track. The place looked very modern and was a nice surprise in my Middle East surroundings. I sat down in the patio and watched a few go-karts zoom around. Overhearing a group of guys speaking English with an American accent, I listened for a while waiting for the right time to approach them and introduce myself. I quickly realized they were in the military, so decided to thank them for their service. These guys were great! Excited to meet a fellow American and interested why a civilian was in Iraq, they invited me to hang out with them. The next day I was picked up from my apartment in an armored car and taken to the base.

The Military Police gave my new friend a hard time about bringing civilians onto the base, but he argued that I was an American and should be allowed in. So he pulled rank and got me in. But that was not the end of it. A high-ranking officer found out and had the MPs pick us up. I was scared as I stood at attention in front of the officer.

At age 19 I never thought I would be questioned before such an officer. He asked me if I was an American. I replied, 'Yes, sir.' Then he asked me if my friend, who was standing next to me, had brought me on base. I replied, 'Yes, sir.' The officer looked at me and asked, 'Is all you can say, "Yes, sir"?' I of course answered, 'Yes, sir.' The officer laughed and asked me a few more questions. Finally, I was able to manage more than a 'Yes, sir.' I explained that I was a Christian sharing my faith and would be in the country for another few weeks.

The next question caught me off guard. 'What can I do for you?' he asked. I was confused and looked at my friend. He shrugged his shoulders and said, 'Tell him what you want.' So I asked for permission to visit his base. He nodded. 'Anything else?' he asked. 'A place to hang out. . .? I don't know', I said with a shaky voice. He chuckled and told my friend to figure it out and dismissed us from his presence.

After that providential meeting I was granted access to the base and given a small office to use. I was constantly picked up and driven around in an armored vehicle. Here I was—out of my depth. I was about the same age as most of the guys so I spent much of my time listening, praying, and sharing my faith with them. God set me up to meet the right guy who would take me to the right place at the right time to meet the right man who could open doors for me."

Reflection Questions

Who was Sergius Paulus, and why was his providential meeting with Paul and Barnabas important to the story?

What is the geographical significance of Paphos as it relates to the possible original destination of the journey?

Where is Pisidian Antioch? What was its strategic importance in the first century?

Why did John Mark leave Paul and Barnabas at Perga? Was his departure justified?

Can you recall a providential meeting that the Holy Spirit used to guide you?

LESSON 7

God uses adversity to guide us.

⁴⁹ The word of the Lord spread through the whole region. ⁵⁰ But the Jewish leaders incited the God-fearing women of high standing and the leading men of the city. They stirred up persecution against Paul and Barnabas, and expelled them from their region. ⁵¹ So they shook the dust off their feet as a warning to them and went to Iconium . . . . ⁴ The people of the city were divided; some sided with the Jews, others with the apostles. ⁵ There was a plot afoot among both Gentiles and Jews, together with their leaders, to mistreat them and stone them. ⁶ But they found out about it and fled to the Lycaonian cities of Lystra and Derbe and to the surrounding country, ⁷ where they continued to preach the gospel . . . .
¹⁹ Then some Jews came from Antioch and Iconium and won the crowd over. They stoned Paul and dragged him outside the city, thinking he was dead. ²⁰ But after the disciples had gathered around him, he got up and went back into the city. The next day he and Barnabas left for Derbe . . . . ²² "We must go through many hardships to enter the kingdom of God," they said. (13:49–51; 14:4–7, 19–20, 22)

Paul's Guidance

From Perga Paul and Barnabas made the 150-mile journey along the Via Sebaste to Pisidian Antioch (Yalvaç). The journey across the Taurus Mountains would take approximately ten days. At Pisidian Antioch Paul preached his first and longest sermon in Acts. His audience in the synagogue consisted both of Jews and Godfearers, that is, Gentiles interested in the God of Israel (13:16–47). Archaeologists have not yet found evidence of a synagogue building in the city.

When they preached in the synagogue again a week later, their message of good news was received by many including even Gentiles. In fact, the word about Jesus Christ also began to circulate in the rural districts surrounding the Roman colony. However, the synagogue leaders, who opposed the message of Jesus and grew jealous of the apostles' favor with the people, incited the elite citizens to expel Paul and Barnabas from Antioch (13:50). Although anticipating opposition at some point, the apostles had probably hoped to remain there longer.

So the two men walked 92 miles eastward along the Via Sebaste to the important Greco-Roman city of Iconium (Konya). Again they preached in the synagogue, and many Jews and Gentiles responded positively to their message. The two were able to stay longer in Iconium than in Pisidian Antioch, and miracles and wonders confirmed their preaching there. But opposition again arose among their opponents, and a plot to stone them was hatched (14:4). Learning of this threat, the apostles fled from Iconium.

They traveled just 21 miles southwestward into the region of Lycaonia to a small Roman colony on the Via Sebaste called Lystra (Hatunsaray). Here their ministry was marked by a dramatic healing: a lame man jumped up and walked at Paul's command. Instantly Paul and Barnabas were hailed as the gods Hermes and Zeus by the locals shouting in the indigenous Lycaonian language. Soon word of the apostles' ministry in Lystra reached the ears of Jews from Antioch who were visiting the synagogue in Iconium. These two groups joined forces and made the short trip to incite the Lystrans against the apostles. They stoned Paul, then dragged him out of the city where they left him for dead (14:19). The irony is striking: days before the apostles were acclaimed as gods; now they were the enemy. The faith of the new local believers was strong: they gathered around Paul and prayed for him. Miraculously, he arose and returned into the city under the believers' protection. The following day he and Barnabas departed for Derbe (14:20).

In the summer of 2016 I traveled along the Via Sebaste with Bob Wagner, who has spent many years tracing the routes of Paul in Turkey. We traced the probable route that led from Lystra to Derbe (Ekinözü). In the first century it passed through a number of small settlements before arriving in the major city of Laranda (Karaman), unmentioned in Acts.

Apparently the apostles only passed through this regional center en route to the smaller city of Derbe fifteen miles to the northeast. Luke does not tell us why their journey ended in Derbe. Perhaps someone from Derbe was visiting Lystra and became a believer after hearing Paul. Gaius from Derbe later was Paul's travel companion (20:4), so maybe it was he who invited Paul to his home to recover after the stoning.

Paul experienced multiple hardships in three Galatian cities during this journey. Yet he did not shun the adversity that had now landed them in Derbe. Luke perhaps gives the impression that Paul went unscathed through these trials. Writing later to his Galatian audience in these churches, he said, "As you know, it was because of a physical infirmity[1] that I first preached the gospel to you, and even though my physical infirmity was a trial to you, you did not treat me with contempt or scorn. Instead, you welcomed me as if I were an angel of God, as if I were Christ Jesus himself. What has happened to all your joy? I can testify that, if you could have done so, you would have torn out your eyes and given them to me" (Gal 4:13–15).

When Paul arrived in Derbe, he was undoubtedly still bruised from the stoning on his head and body. These would be evident to everyone in the city. It seems that an additional result of the stoning was damage to his vision. A frequent effect of traumatic brain injury (TBI) is sight impairment including visual acuity loss and visual field loss.[2] Apparently he struggled with sight issues for a period after the stoning so that believers in Lystra, Iconium, and Pisidian Antioch were aware of this debility (Gal 4:15). We don't know when the physical signs of the stoning ended, but it seems Paul did regain full use of his vision again. Adversity was a factor in guidance at least three times during the first journey, and it also impacted Paul's physical well-being.

1. I have changed the NIV translation here from "illness." The Greek word *astheneia* covers any sort of physical weakness including sickness and debility (see John 5:5). Using "illness" already suggests a choice of interpretation for Paul's condition, which I suggest otherwise in my comments.

2. Further discussion of such sight problems can be found at Goodrich, "Vision Issues."

Guidance Today

Thankfully, neither Dindy nor I have experienced much adversity in our lives. As baby boomers, our generation has lived through one of the most prosperous periods in American history. Our parents had experienced the Great Depression and World War II, but these were their memories, not ours. Jobs were abundant, educational levels rose, prosperity flourished. Trials in our family have been minimal. My paternal grandfather Tony died in a tractor accident when I was eleven. Dindy's parents, Albert and Florence, both died when she was in her early 20s, so I never met either of them. When my maternal grandparents, Bill and Agnes, died in 1992 both in their 90s, a generous bequest in their will provided the down payment to buy our first home. Fortunately, our children and grandchildren have never suffered any major illnesses or injuries. My greatest physical challenge has been two surgeries on my nose to remove basal cell carcinoma. So "suffering for Jesus" at its worst has been when a car broke down or a refrigerator quit running. However, over the years we have known and supported many friends who have experienced adversities such as severe illness, tragic accident, or financial loss.

Jackson Crum writes:

"My wife Donna and I had a three and a half month-old son die of Sudden Infant Death Syndrome (SIDS). To say we were devastated would be a serious understatement. I had never known pain like that before or since.

I battled between what I knew to be true and what I felt. It seemed so unfair to me. I was pastoring at the time and had this underlying belief God owed me more. Wasn't I sacrificing enough already? Why did you take my son? For months I struggled with being able to believe God was good. I knew it to be true theologically, but my emotions said, 'God could not be trusted.' All the while I am pastoring, teaching and shepherding. I felt like such a hypocrite.

One morning I knew I had to get this settled with God one way or the other. I got in my car and drove to Valley Forge National Park outside of Philadelphia. I was going to have it out with God once and for all. At the park I got out the car and began to walk. I was not leaving the park until I came to some kind of understanding with God. I was hurt, mad, and confused.

I had started walking toward a trail when I heard a voice so clear that I turned around to see who was behind me. But no one was there. I heard God say to me, 'What have I called you to do?' I replied quietly out loud, 'To love and obey you.' God then said to me, 'That's right. Now go home.'

I returned to my car and drove away. Believe it or not, that was all I heard and that was all I needed to hear. God needed to remind me that there were some things I would never understand, but he was still God. I was reminded of Job's conversation with God at the end of Job. God never gave Job a reason; he just reminded him that God was God and he was not."

Martyrdom in Malatya:

From my years of teaching Revelation, I've thought a lot about persecution—a theme running through the book. In chapters 2 and 3 believers in Smyrna, Pergamum, and Philadelphia all experienced adversity. John later saw a great multitude from every nation who had come out of the great tribulation (Rev 7:14). To help increase the awareness of Western Christians concerning the issue of persecution, I included an account of martyrdom at the beginning of each chapter in my book, *Victory through the Lamb*.

In Izmir we attended the Lighthouse Church that used to meet in a building with a large window looking toward the acropolis of Smyrna. Each Sunday I reflected on Polycarp and his death in the stadium there in 156 CE. The *Martyrdom of Polycarp* records that before his arrest while the bishop was praying, he fell into a trance and saw his pillow being consumed by fire. He turned to those who were with him and stated, 'It is necessary that I be burned alive" (*Mart. of Poly.* 5.1–2, Holmes trans.). Three days later he was led into the stadium to be burned on a pyre. After he prayed, the fire was lit, but instead of his body being consumed, bystanders witnessed a miracle. Rather than burnt flesh, the smell was "like bread baking or like gold and silver being refined in a furnace. For we also perceived a very fragrant odor, as if it were like the scent of incense or some other precious spice" (*Mart. of Poly.* 15.2, Holmes trans.). Realizing that the fire was not going to consume Polycarp, his executioner stabbed him with a dagger. The vision God had given Polycarp beforehand prepared him spiritually and psychologically for his approaching death.

Three years after moving to Turkey, Dindy and I were part of the Christian community that was stunned by the brutal murder of three believers in Malatya. Martyrdom was no longer an abstract academic subject for me, but a painful existential reality. At the funeral and interment of Necati Aydın in Izmir, we shared in the grief and loss experienced by family members and friends. A later memorial service for all three martyrs in Izmir's Anglican Church reminded local believers again of the sacrifice that these brothers had made. Here is the story of these martyrs, particularly Tilmann Geske.

Even before their wedding in 1992, Tilmann and Susanne Geske agreed that they wanted to live in a Muslim country in the future. As Tilmann was completing a five-year pastoral commitment at their church in Germany, the two begin to pray for guidance about the future. Tilmann wanted to move to Indonesia while Susanne preferred Turkey. Since they couldn't agree, they began to consider a compromise—Iran. When they heard about a local Bible college organizing a trip to Iran, they decided to join to investigate that possibility further. However, the group needed four more people for the trip to proceed. In the interim Tilmann and Susanne individually read about a proposed prayer journey to eastern Turkey. Comparing notes, they together realized that their interest in participating in this trip was greater than the one to Iran. Shortly after, the Iranian trip leader called with news that the trip had been cancelled. The decision was settled: Turkey would be their destination.

However, their first trip to Turkey was somewhat of a disaster. Both were sick the entire time with Susanne, also pregnant, being so weak that Tilmann had to carry her about. Their friends who conducted the trip thought that the Geskes would never return to Turkey because of their horrible first experience there. However, their call was confirmed, and after a time of preparation the Geskes moved to Adana in 1997. After a season of language study and acculturation there, the Geske family decided in 2002 to move further east to Malatya. This is the background behind the tragic events of April 18, 2007.

Tilmann with two Muslim-background Turkish believers, Necati Aydın and Uğur Yüksel, worked for a small Christian publishing company called Zirve. In 2005 trouble had started in Malatya when protestors claimed that Zirve's Bible and literature distribution was proselytizing the local people. They demanded that Zirve be closed. However, under Turkish law, the right to evangelize is legally guaranteed. Necati also served as pastor of the local Kurtuluş (Salvation) Church where those interested in learning about Christianity would visit. But in the early months of 2007 Zirve's workers began to receive numerous death threats.

On the morning of April 18, 2007, Yunus Emre Günaydın along with four young men entered Zirve's office. Günaydın had been a regular visitor to the publishing office for Bible studies, so was known to Necati, Uğur, and Tilmann. However, this time he and his friends had other sinister plans so they tied the three Christians to their chairs and threatened them. Other Turkish believers Gökhan Talas and his wife later came to the office, only to find its door locked from the inside. Suspecting something was wrong, Talas called Uğur. In an attempt to protect Talas and his wife, Uğur said they were at a hotel for a meeting. When Talas heard someone crying in the background, he called the police who arrived shortly afterwards. When the police began to storm the office, the kidnappers attacked their victims. The three Christians were found with their hands and feet tied and throats cut; their bodies had multiple stab wounds. Necati and Tilmann were already dead, but Uğur was still breathing. He was rushed to a nearby hospital, but even massive blood transfusions were unable to save his life.

Günaydın, the instigator of the murders, was seriously injured when he jumped three stories to the street below while attempting to escape. The other four, still holding their bloody knives, were taken into custody as they tried to flee the building. The murderers were carrying a note that read, "We did it for our country. They are trying to take our country away, take our religion away." Under interrogation, they admitted that Necati, Uğur, and Tilmann were killed as a lesson to other Christians regarding what would happen to enemies of their religion in Turkey. Adversity had struck the church in Turkey, and the memory of their sacrifice lives on until today.[3]

Reflection Questions

What kind of adversity did Paul and Barnabas experience on this journey?

Who initiated this persecution, and why?

How did the apostles respond to their mistreatment in these Galatian cities?

Why were the apostles stoned in Lystra, and what was the result?

Have you encountered serious adversity in life? If so, how did God guide you through it?

3. Summarized from Carswell, *Married*, 36–63, and Wilson, *Victory*, 197–99.

LESSON 8

God uses a sense of duty to guide us.

[21] Then they returned to Lystra, Iconium and Antioch, [22] strengthening the disciples and encouraging them to remain true to the faith . . .. [23] Paul and Barnabas appointed elders for them in each church and, with prayer and fasting, committed them to the Lord, in whom they had put their trust. [24] After going through Pisidia, they came into Pamphylia, [25] and when they had preached the word in Perga, they went down to Attalia. (14:21–25)

Paul's Guidance

Adversity had brought Paul and Barnabas to Derbe, the easternmost city in their first journey. A glance at the map of this journey shows that Tarsus, Paul's home, was only 130 miles away. Antioch was only another week's journey farther. In fact, on his second and third journeys Paul took this direct route to Derbe north from Tarsus[1] and through the Cilician Gates, the main pass in the Taurus Mountains. If I were in Paul's shoes, I would have said to myself, "Enough is enough; it's time to return to Antioch, report on our ministry successes, and get some R&R." However, he and Barnabas didn't do this; they decided to return to the very cities from which they had been rejected, ejected, and stoned. What prompted this decision? They felt a sense of duty to the new believers in them. Without adequate spiritual leadership, Paul realized that these churches might not survive.

1. The well-preserved section of road north of Tarsus is depicted in Michael Holter's illustration for the cover of this book.

Paul changed hats from being a church-planting apostle to a care-giving pastor. So he and Barnabas retraced their steps to Lystra, Iconium, and Pisidian Antioch. Whether they incurred any further opposition from local synagogue leaders upon their return is not mentioned. Instead the focus is on the appointment of elders in each church. The NIV footnote for verse 23 suggests that the Greek word *cheirontoneō* could also be translated "ordained" or "elected."

One important duty to which the early church repeatedly gave attention was the selection of mature leaders. This process occurred in various ways. After the apostles prayed for guidance in choosing a replacement for Judas, Matthias was selected as the twelfth apostle through the casting of lots (1:26). The church in Jerusalem chose, probably by election, seven deacons to oversee the distribution of food to the widows and needy (6:1–6). After the Jerusalem council the apostles, elders, and believers in Jerusalem chose Judas and Silas to accompany Paul and Barnabas back to Antioch with the letter announcing their decision (15:22, 25). How the selection of the two was made is unstated, but they were probably a consensus choice ratified by a voice vote or show of hands. In each of these four texts the Greek word *eklegomai* ("to select") is used, which shows the range of methods by which leaders were selected in the early church. Thus it is inaccurate to say that Acts shows a single, normative method for choosing leaders.

Paul had grown up in the synagogue, and the Jewish community's way of selecting leaders must have influenced his own perspective. In Pisidian Antioch it was the synagogue rulers who had invited Paul and Barnabas to speak. Inscriptions tells us that this important office was held by influential, educated persons chosen by the local Jewish community. They were also persons of financial means who could serve as benefactors for the synagogue as well.

One question arising from the appointment of elders in the Galatian churches is that it seems to violate a principle later elaborated by Paul: "Do not be hasty in the laying on of hands" (1 Tim 5:22). Weren't these men chosen within weeks of their newly found faith in Jesus? Indeed they were, but all were also mature heads of families and most probably leaders in their local synagogues. They also had a knowledge of the Jewish Scriptures, and all except the Godfearers would have been circumcised as sons of the covenant. So they were very different from the Gentiles to whom Paul was writing in 1 Timothy. These Gentile believers had recently come out of paganism with little foundation in monotheistic Judaism or knowledge of the Jewish Scriptures.

At the beginning of the journey Paul and Barnabas had stopped briefly in Perga before pressing on to Pisidian Antioch. At that time they had probably made contact with the Jewish community and promised to return and reason with them about Jesus (as later in Ephesus; 18:19–21). If that were the case, their return to Perga was another instance of duty motivating their decision. As mentioned earlier, the journey by road to Antioch was shorter and through familiar territory. However, the apostles apparently took a more direct but unfamiliar route through the rugged Taurus Mountains of Pisidia back to Perga. Then a voyage by ship was required from Pamphylia back to Antioch, a land and sea journey approximately 20 per cent longer than overland.

The phrase "to speak the word" is used six times in Acts (4:29, 31; 8:25; 11:19; 13:46; 15:36) with its near equivalent "to preach the word" used eight times (5:42; 8:4; 11:20; 14:7, 35; 15:35; 16:6, 32). Once there is "to announce the word" (13:5) and another time "teaching the word" (18:11). In each example there is an expressed or anticipated positive result to Paul's message. However, at Perga Luke does not mention that believers resulted from his preaching. This failure to mention a church plant is likewise absent in Salamis (13:5). The fact that Barnabas and John Mark later returned suggests there was a church to revisit (15:39). Since Acts shows repeatedly that converts resulted from Paul's preaching, it should be assumed that some came to faith in Perga and also possibly in nearby Attalia.

Guidance Today

In April 2011 I was finishing up my service as interim pastor at the Union Church of Istanbul. Dindy and I had been praying about where to live next and decided to relocate to Antalya. So after the Easter service at UCI, we flew to our new home. Pastor James Bultema and his wife Renata had graciously offered their empty bedroom while we searched for an apartment. Through their friend who was a realtor, we found an older three-bedroom apartment with a lovely Mediterranean seaview. It was within walking distance to the old city Kaleiçi and convenient to the bus routes, an important consideration since we don't have a car in Turkey.

In the midst of this transition, my sister informed me that our father Wayne had suffered a heart attack and died in North Dakota. Dad was 89 years old, and a believer who had lived a rich and full life. We were expecting him to live until 90 and already planning his birthday party. I immediately booked a flight back to the United States and left Dindy to make the transition into our new apartment. As the eldest of three children, I felt it my duty to be present for our father's funeral, at which I spoke. I also presided at his interment at the cemetery in Braham, Minnesota, where all of my family members are buried. I also tried to be a source of encouragement and comfort to our stepmother Idella. The timing of Dad's death was not convenient; many things that happen in life aren't convenient. Dindy had to sort out many details related to our relocation. But God gave us grace during this time of grieving and stress, and thankfully every detail fell into place.

Back in the 1980s when Dindy and I were in graduate school, I worked full-time as a commissioned salesman at Montgomery Ward (see Lesson 18). The job was ideal because its flexible hours allowed me to build a schedule around class and family needs. Like all parents, we were committed to supporting our children in their various extracurricular activities. Our sons played soccer, and their games were usually on Saturday mornings. So when their games happened, I scheduled myself for a late shift that day. The challenge was that Saturday morning was the highest-volume sales period of the week, and I was not working at that time. Yet I felt it my parental duty to be on the sidelines cheering for my sons. Nevertheless, God honored that decision repeatedly by bringing in large-ticket tire sales on Saturday evenings and other times so that my salary was seldom affected.

When Dindy and I moved to Turkey in 2004, we made the decision to return annually to America to visit our children and grandchildren. Despite telephone and internet connections, we felt it significant that they see us in person each year. So every fall we make the trek back to spend two months shuttling from Seattle to western Virginia to see our extended family. I must also conduct annual board meetings for the two nonprofit organizations that support our work in Turkey. The boards for the Seven Churches Network and the Asia Minor Research Center are comprised of long-time friends—Bob and Bette Biddle, Bob and Janyce O'Brien, Jerry and Margaret Kidd, Jim and Susan Funari, Michael and Cyndy Holter—who give oversight and counsel regarding our organizational activities. Another yearly activity is to attend academic society meetings where I present papers related to my scholarly research. At these meetings I also assist my friend Levent Oral of Tutku Tours in promoting biblical tours to professors and scholars gathered there. Family, business, and scholarship encompass the three areas of duties related to these annual visits to America.

Most of our decisions are not the result of an angelic visitation, prophecy, or dream. Rather they are obedient responses to scriptural teaching to love our spouses unconditionally, rear our children in the fear of the Lord, treat our friends and employees with respect, obey the laws of our country, and gather regularly with other believers. Doing life's mundane duties is not glamorous or exciting for the most part. The "same old, same old" comprises much of our existence. As someone has trenchantly said, "The worst part of daily life is that it's so daily." Donald Gee summarizes the temptation to circumvent this: "There is scarcely anything more nauseating than professing to receive some personal 'revelation' that flatly contradicts the ordinary, decent, and Scriptural duties of everyday life."[2] We should not be dismayed when our daily planners are largely filled with mundane activities, since God's good and pleasing and perfect will (Rom 12:2) usually consists of such basic duties.

Eugene Jahn writes:

"We have an adult son with disabilities who has lived with us since birth. He needs services to assist him in obtaining and maintaining a job in addition to other services which will teach him independent living skills. We were unsuccessful in finding these much-needed services in Virginia. During the past several years, we have searched other states in an effort to locate the necessary services that he requires. Finally, we identified Colorado as a state willing to provide these services for our son. However, Michael was not eligible to apply for Medicaid in Colorado until we physically moved to this state.

In 2016 my wife Charlotte and I decided to move from Virginia Beach to Colorado Springs. Having lived in Virginia for 33 ½ years, it took months to close down our house. It was difficult to move from the area, particularly since we were leaving our daughter and her family of eight children behind. We finally left Virginia in early July and drove 1800 miles cross country arriving in Colorado Springs ten days later. After establishing residency in Colorado, we submitted a Medicaid application for Michael. It was approved ten days later. We are so thankful for the Lord's provision

---

2. Gee, *Studies in Guidance*, 44.

which includes the services that Michael has now been receiving for the past several months. However, it was so important for us to make the move to enable our son to receive the services that he so desperately needed."

Reflection Questions

Why did Paul return to the cities where he had experienced adverse treatment?

How were Paul and Barnabas guided in selecting leaders to oversee the new churches?

Have you ever been involved in choosing church leaders? If so, describe how the Holy Spirit helped to guide you in making the decision?

What Christian duties are presently guiding the decisions you are making?

4

The Second Journey

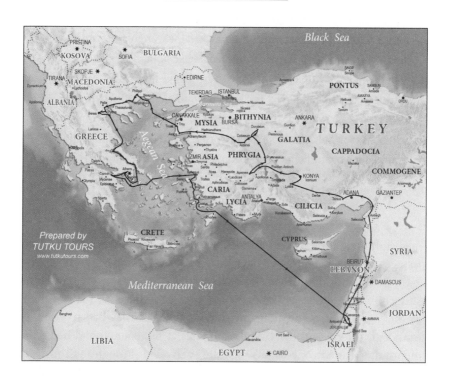

Lesson 9

God uses conflict to guide us.

³⁶ Some time later Paul said to Barnabas, "Let us go back and visit the believers in all the towns where we preached the word of the Lord and see how they are doing." ³⁷ Barnabas wanted to take John, also called Mark, with them, ³⁸ but Paul did not think it wise to take him, because he had deserted them in Pamphylia and had not continued with them in the work. ³⁹ They had such a sharp disagreement that they parted company. Barnabas took Mark and sailed for Cyprus, ⁴⁰ but Paul chose Silas and left, commended by the believers to the grace of the Lord. (15:36–40)

Paul's Guidance

The beginning of the second journey presents one of the most perplexing passages in Acts. Lessons 2–8 have linked Paul predominantly with Barnabas—his mentor and friend. The two served as leaders in the church in Antioch, ministered together in Cyprus and Asia Minor, and risked their lives in various cities for the name of Jesus (15:26). They had traveled to Jerusalem to represent the Gentile churches at the council and had won important spiritual concessions regarding salvation through faith instead of circumcision and keeping the law. The leaders in Jerusalem had tasked them with conveying the council's results in a letter to the Gentile churches (15:23–29). After delivering the letter in Antioch and teaching about its theological implications for Christian living, Paul and Barnabas began to make plans to deliver it to churches in Syria and Cilicia as well as to revisit the churches in Galatia and to check the spiritual progress of believers there.

But something that happened in Pamphylia on the first journey proved problematic for their ongoing collaboration. At Perga John Mark had left Paul and Barnabas to return to Jerusalem. Various explanations for this "desertion" have been offered. One is homesickness; another a failure of courage when he saw the rugged Taurus Mountains. A third suggests that he was offended by Paul taking the lead, indicated by his name now mentioned first (13:13). The most likely reason, mentioned in Lesson 6, is that when the direction shifted from North Africa to Asia Minor, John Mark became unhappy with this change of plan. His interest was evangelizing Egypt and Cyrene so he decided to jump ship, so to speak.

Paul didn't think it would be a "wise" decision to take John Mark along again. The Greek verb *axioō* used here suggests a preference or opinion, and clearly Paul had one on this matter. But Barnabas had a different one, and as an encourager, he was willing to forgive and forget this act of immaturity by his cousin (Col 4:10). But Paul saw no reason to include someone who had deserted them once and might do so again. Perhaps he was also thinking that the churches in Galatia, hearing about John Mark's earlier desertion, might question Paul's judgment for including him on this mission. So Paul and Barnabas reached an impasse regarding John Mark's inclusion on the second journey.

Oh to be a fly on the wall listening to their conversation! What might it have been like—two men full of the Holy Spirit (9:17; 11:24)—raising their voices in defense of their positions? Was John Mark in the room with them, or did they have the wisdom to send him out before things got heated? Luke uses the rare Greek word *paroxusmos* to describe their contention. Stronger than just being angry or upset, it suggests a sharp argument or disagreement. If there is any such thing as "arguing in the Spirit," this must have been the occasion. The result was that these men of God—friends for almost two decades—parted company to go their separate ways.

Luke is brutally honest in his portrayal of the early church, warts and all. He described how Ananias and Sapphira withheld money from their land sale and died in judgment as a lesson for others (5:1–11). After his baptism by Philip, Simon tried to buy the gift of the Holy Spirit from Peter and John (8:9–24). And Jewish believers from Jerusalem began to teach a different gospel in Antioch stating that circumcision was necessary for salvation (15:1). Sometimes believers today lament that that we need to get back to the early church as seen in Acts. Where are the miracles, signs, and wonders today, they ask? But conveniently left out is the other half of the picture. The early church didn't operate continuously on some exalted "Holy Ghost" plane; it struggled with issues such lying, greed, and false teaching too.

This falling-out between two heroes of the early church must have come as a shock to Luke's first audience. The result is unfortunate because Barnabas now disappears in Acts never to show his face again, while Paul continues as the dominant character. Their disagreement occurred just as departure time approached, but providentially for Paul a prophet named Silas was in Antioch. The Jerusalem church had previously sent Silas as one of its representative to Antioch (15:32); then he and Judas had returned to Jerusalem to report about the letter's positive reception. Apparently Silas was led by the Spirit to return to Antioch, and thus was available to go with Paul after the split. Barnabas took John Mark, and the two sailed to Cyprus to revisit the churches there. On this occasion they probably reached the first journey's original destination—Alexandria. Despite this sharp dis-agreement, God was still able to accomplish his divine plan: two ministry journeys now left Antioch instead of one.

Luke never describes a reconciliation between Paul and Barnabas. Nevertheless, Paul himself suggests that such a rapprochement did occur. Writing to the Corinthians years later from Ephesus, Paul noted that he and Barnabas were examples of apostles who worked for a living (1 Cor 9:6). If and when Barnabas visited Corinth is not known, but Paul cited him as a positive example for the believers there. Later Paul reconciled with John Mark too. From his Roman imprisonment he asked the Colossian church to welcome John Mark if he should visit (Col. 4:10). The mindset of unity—one purpose and one accord (*homothumadon*) that Luke repeatedly cites as a virtue of the early believers (1:14; 2:46; 4:24; 5:12; 15:25)—was once again realized among Paul, Barnabas, and John Mark.

Guidance Today

The voice on the other end of the line was a reporter from the *Tulsa World* requesting to interview me. He wanted to discuss Tim LaHaye's Left Behind series and its popularity with Christians. I asked how he had obtained my name; he replied that the public relations department at Oral Roberts University had provided it. Since I was the main faculty member teaching on eschatology and Revelation, the PR folks thought I was the "go to guy" for an interview on the subject.

I arranged a meeting time with the reporter, and we had a productive discussion about the various views that evangelicals held about the so-called "End Times." I noted that LaHaye's pretribulional, premillennial perspective represented only part of the Christian community, and that a full range of views was taught in my class at ORU. Having learned the dangers of being misquoted, I asked the reporter to see a draft of his article before it was published. He kindly assented, and I was happy with his story that ran in the newspaper that weekend.

Monday morning I received a call from the academic dean's office requesting that I meet with the dean. Puzzled as to the reason, I nevertheless made an appointment. At the meeting the dean told me that an ORU board meeting had read the article and was upset by my comments. He apparently was a big LaHaye supporter and was concerned that a faculty member was teaching what he perceived might be "deviant" views about Revelation and eschatology. I got a bit defensive, feeling I'd been setup by ORU's own PR department. My point to the dean was that if this was a university, all credible viewpoints needed to be taught. My meeting concluded with a caution to watch my public comments in the future. I left fuming inside.

Some months later I organized a trip to Turkey, and around twenty students signed up. It was originally to be sponsored by my Seven Churches Network, but the university decided it should come under its umbrella for insurance reasons. I soon began to have a bad feeling about this arrange-ment. On the morning of October 12, 2000—the day the travel company required an initial deposit—I walked into the faculty offices. Our depart-ment secretary Susan said that the deans wanted to meet with me about the trip. Surprised, I asked, "What for?" She said that the news about the bombing of the U.S.S. Cole had them concerned. I was flabbergasted and observed that 1800 miles separated Yemen from Turkey. Since I had classes to teach that morning, I suggested a meeting after lunch.

After my classes were completed, I found Susan and asked when and where the meeting was to be held. She said there would be no meeting; the decision had already been made to cancel the trip. As an unemotional Swede, I remained calm on the outside but inside I was going ballistic. All the work I had put into organizing the trip was for naught. I stormed out of the building, probably the most upset I've ever been in my life, and called Dindy to vent about the decision. The conflict surrounding those two in-cidents figured prominently in my decision to resign the following spring (see Lesson 13).

While conflict in churches, universities, and ministries is regrettable, it is inevitable. How we as believers resolve such conflict should distinguish us from how unbelievers handle disagreement. Unfortunately godly virtues do not always prevail, and our Christian witness can be adversely impacted. Even though reconciliation cannot always occur, we must strive for it even as Paul did.

Mark D. Roberts writes:

"About fifteen years ago I was in the midst of one of the hardest times in my ministry at Irvine Presbyterian Church. I had a staff member I'll call Shirley with whom I was having many conflicts. From my point of view, she was not fulfilling her job description in many, many ways. From her point of view, I was being imperious and unsupportive. Though I tried everything I could think of to make things work out, they were going south faster than a goose in November.

During this time, Shirley began to lobby the troops on her side. She complained about how I was mistreating her. She would visit shut-ins and tell them I was getting ready to fire her (which wasn't true). She was clearly trying to divide the church and was doing a fine job of it. I must confess that I was sorely tempted to join the game and beat her at it. I wanted to get people on my side. I wanted people to know the truth and defend me. The church started to become all about me, . . . me, me, me. We were going the way of the splintered Corinthian church.

Everything came to a head at a meeting of our congregation. This was by far the toughest meeting I'd ever been a part of. The elders of the church were recommending that we dismiss Shirley from our staff. In the congregational debate, many people chewed me out for what they perceived to be my management flaws. These were people who believed they knew the truth because they had heard it from Shirley. The temptation to divide and conquer the church was huge for me.

But, by God's grace and following the counsel of my fellow leaders, I didn't do it. I took my licks, even ones I didn't deserve. I owned my failures and tried to listen to what people were saying to me. Frankly, it was excruciating. But I sensed that my job as pastor was to help the church be unified in Christ, not divided in order to defend me. Many of my supporters sensed the same. Though they could have risen to my defense, they realized that it was not the time to do so. Wisely, they remained quiet, and so avoided a fight that could have deeply wounded our church.

The congregation did, in the end, vote to dismiss Shirley. I left feeling, not vindicated, but ashamed and exhausted. Several friends gathered around to encourage me. But I still felt as if I had been taken to the congregational woodshed for a beating. In the aftermath of that meeting, only a couple of people left our church, much to my surprise. In time, many of those who had scolded me actually came to apologize. One man said, 'It was only later that I learned some of what had really happened with Shirley. I'm sorry for the things I said to you.'

But the greatest result of that whole debacle was not that I was somehow more highly regarded or more beloved or whatever. It was that our people ended up, truly, more united in Christ. I can't explain how this happened, exactly, except that it was a work of grace. But I do know that my effort, and the efforts of those who supported me, to focus on Christ and not on me helped move us toward such a positive result. Nevertheless, I still look back on this whole experience, and the congregational meeting in particular, as one of the hardest times of my ministry. It required that I subordinate myself to a degree I had never done before. It required that I trust in God rather than my abilities to persuade and organize."[1]

Reflection Questions

What was the cause of the disagreement compelling Paul and Barnabas to separate?

Is either party to be blamed for it, and do you think their parting was justified?

What role did Silas and later Timothy play in the second journey?

Were there any long-term effects resulting from this conflict?

Have you ever experienced conflict that influenced your course of action?

1. Roberts, "God's Guidance," and used with permission.

LESSON 10

God uses closed doors to guide us.

⁶ Paul and his companions traveled throughout the region of Phrygia and
Galatia, having been kept by the Holy Spirit from preaching the word in
the province of Asia. ⁷ When they came to the border of Mysia, they tried
to enter Bithynia, but the Spirit of Jesus would not allow them to. ⁸ So they
passed by Mysia and went down to Troas. (16:6–8)

Paul's Guidance

So far Luke has shown the Spirit positively directing the spread of the gospel outward from Jerusalem (1:8, 8:29, 39; 10:19–20; 13:2–4). Suddenly
the Spirit is giving negative directions to Paul. A related question in these
verses is whether Luke is making some theological distinction between the
"Holy Spirit" and the "Spirit of Jesus" (cf. Phil 1:19). He appears not to be,
since the divine voice behind both prohibitions is one and the same. Did
these prohibitions come to Paul through natural or supernatural means?
Luke doesn't tell us, but we learned earlier that Silas was a prophet (15:32).
The likelihood is that Silas received prophecies or words of knowledge from
the Spirit that he shared with Paul and Timothy.

These three verses and their context require a brief introduction to the
geography of western Asia Minor and its road system in the first century AD.
So look at the map that begins this chapter.[1] After Paul's disagreement with
Barnabas, he left Antioch with Silas. The two delivered the council's letter to

1. The map was initially prepared to illustrate the article by Thompson and Wilson,
"Route," 244.

the churches in coastal Syria and Plain Cilicia around Tarsus (15:41). He and Silas then visited Derbe, Lystra, and Iconium—the churches started by Paul on the first journey. At Lystra Timothy joined them after his circumcision by Paul (16:1–5). Although Pisidian Antioch is not mentioned, its prominence in Acts with Paul's first recorded speech (13:14–51) suggests that this church was also visited. Since these Christians comprised the primary audience for his letter to the Galatians, Paul wished to inform them personally of the council's decision about circumcision and food laws. His projected route west conveniently led through these four Galatian churches.

The translation of 16:6 is difficult with the best option being "they passed through the region of Phrygian Galatia." Phrygia was a region in central Asia Minor whose boundaries overlapped the Roman provinces of Asia and Galatia. Iconium and Pisidian Antioch were located in the Phrygian part of Galatia. The region west of Pisidian Antioch along the Via Sebaste seems to be the area to which Luke is referring. Paul's destination was apparently Ephesus.

Why Ephesus? It was the fourth largest city in the Roman Empire and the capital of the province of Asia. Ephesus also had a large Jewish population. As the western terminus of the Southern, or Common, Highway, it was a great commercial center with a strategic harbor. It was also a religious center with the temple of Artemis, one of the seven wonders of the ancient world. At nearby Claros an important Apollo oracle temple stood. So Paul was not traveling willy-nilly; he had an intentional strategy to plant churches in key urban centers in the eastern Mediterranean. And the road upon which he was traveling was the most direct route from Iconium to Ephesus.

West of Apollonia, the Via Sebaste turned south towards Perga and the Mediterranean coast, his inbound route on the first journey. However, the Southern Highway continued westward toward the next major road junction at Apamea (Dinar). The boundary between Galatia and Asia, later marked by a monument, stood at the top of a pass. The ancient road descending to the plain below is well preserved near the village of Çapalı. A clear distinction exists between the two prohibitions in Acts 16. The first prohibited the apostolic party from preaching in the province of Asia, while the second did not even allow them to enter the province of Bithynia. During the remainder of their journey until Troas Paul and his companions were always traveling in Asia.

Near Apamea Paul formulated a new plan with a new destination. They decided to turn northward toward Bithynia to evangelize its major cities. Nicomedia was the provincial capital, and Nicea was an important commercial center. Both cities also had a Jewish population. Again Paul was directed by the same strategic purpose. To reach Bithynia, they now turned north toward the next important road junction at Prymnessus (near Afyonkarahisar). Luke provides a clue as to their direction: "they passed along Mysia" (16:7). Mysia was another geographic region in northwestern Asia, and Cotiaeum (Kütahya) was a major city situated near its border. From Cotiaeum the main road to Bithynia led northeast to Dorylaeum (Eskişehir), a major city and transportation hub in north central Asia that stood on the border of Bithynia. At Dorylaeum the second prohibition was probably received, this time from the Spirit of Jesus.

With "Plan B" north into Bithynia now blocked as well, "Plan C" was conceived. The only direction remaining open was westward to the Aegean coast. So they retraced their steps to Cotiaeum and continued to Aezanoi (Çavdarhisar), another major Greco-Roman city. From Aezanoi they continued southwest to Kadi (Eski Gediz) where they turned northwest to Synaos (Simav) and Ancyra Sidera (Boğazköy). Following the Macestus (Simav) River, they reached the next major road junction at Hadrianuthera (Balıkesir). The Aegean coast was a short walk down to Adramyttium (Edremit), another important city in Asia. (On Paul's captivity journey to Rome he was to sail on a ship whose home port was Adramyttium; 27:2). Since they received no further guidance here, the three continued along the northern coastline of the Gulf of Adramyttium past the cities of Antandrus and New Gargara before climbing into the region called the Troad.

Paul now turned west toward Troas, a sea and land transportation hub in northwestern Asia Minor that guarded the entrance to the Hellespont (or Dardanelles), a strait leading to the Black Sea. From the port of Troas there was regular ferry service linking the continent of Asia to Europe. After two previous prohibitions, the apostolic party had finally run out of land; only water lay ahead. Arriving in Troas, their expectations must have been high that God would somehow guide them forward.

This detailed description might have seemed tedious. However, it was necessary to show the immense geographical scope packed into these three verses. Paul traveled over five hundred miles from Syrian Antioch before the first prohibition was received near Apamea. He and his companions continued another 160 miles until the second prohibition was given at Dorylaeum. From Dorylaeum to Troas the journey westward comprised another 325 miles without any guidance. Paul had traveled almost one thousand miles since leaving Syrian Antioch. Since the average travel distance was about twenty miles a day and considering the stops at the Galatian churches, it would have taken them at least three months to reach Troas. During many nights around the campfire the apostles undoubtedly looked at each other, wondering when the Holy Spirit would give them further guidance. Knowing the distances and times involved at this stage of the second journey allows us to appreciate better Paul's patience, obedience, and sensitivity to be guided by the Spirit wherever that might lead.

Guidance Today

As I neared graduation in 1982 from Trinity Bible College in Ellendale, North Dakota, Dindy and I began to pray about our next step. As part of my practical ministry at TBC, I was involved in outreach to Native Americans. Living on the Pine Ridge Reservation had given us a love for Indian people, and we enjoyed ministering to them. The president of the Good Shepherd Bible Institute (later Central Indian Bible College) invited me to come and teach at its campus in Mobridge, SD. Although I was not ordained in the Assemblies of God, the district superintendent supported my call to GSBI and approved me to raise support among the AG churches in North and South Dakota and Montana.

I taught a variety of classes and thoroughly enjoyed my interaction with the students. However, the prospect of long-term teaching was dim because of my inability to be ordained. The reason: Dindy had been divorced. Even though I was the one seeking ordination and Dindy's divorce was prior to her salvation, the denomination's bylaws forbade my ordination. We were advised by colleagues that we had no future in the AG and that we should begin to look elsewhere for ministry. I had begun part-time graduate study, so we started to look for a school to begin full-time study. In this context, the Lord led us to move to Virginia (see Lesson 6). Surely our lives might have been different if the door to ministry in the Assemblies of God had not been closed.

Fast forward to 2004. In preparation for our move to Turkey, we were searching for a residence to serve as our home base. We had sold our house in Tulsa so had some equity that needed to be reinvested in another property. For months we had searched the web sites of realtors, read the want ads in the Virginian Pilot, and driven the streets of Norfolk, Virginia, looking for FSBOs (For Sale by Owner). We were living in a rental house situated on the Chesapeake Bay, but soon discovered that our pockets were not deep enough to purchase even a condominium or apartment near the beach. Plus we didn't want to worry about protecting a beach property whenever a hurricane threatened the mid-Atlantic coast.

Because Norfolk has so many waterfront properties, we began to look farther inland along its bays and inlets. Driving to work one day, Dindy saw a small house in a nice neighborhood that fit our criteria. We were looking for a low-maintenance property with a small yard, something that we could lock up and forget about while we were in Turkey. We made an offer on the house, and it was accepted so we arranged a loan through our bank. We paid for the initial inspection, and the closing for the sale was contingent on correcting a few minor problems. Everything looked promising as we moved forward with the purchase.

Then the heavens opened, and it rained hard for several days. When we went for the final inspection, the basement was flooded with two feet of standing water. Because the area was tidal, we learned that basements in the area often flooded unless a sump pump had been installed. However, the owners of this property had never installed such a pump. We were devastated; months of searching had brought us to this house. And it proved unlivable without an additional financial investment that we didn't have. After praying, Dindy and I accepted that God had closed the door on this house so we withdrew our offer. Reluctantly we agreed that God must have something better.

So our property search began anew; however, time was running out before our scheduled departure. For several weeks a co-op apartment had been advertised in the paper. Since we were focused on finding a house, we hadn't followed up on it. As we prayed, Dindy kept picturing a brick apartment building so we decided to check out this place called Camellia Court. Sure enough it was an older brick apartment complex! The advertised apartment was unavailable for viewing that Sunday; however, the manager mentioned that there was another apartment for sale in the building. Its owner worked abroad for the State Department. The apartment had stood empty for five years after its renovation following a fire. Upon seeing its oak floors and lovely high ceilings with an open floor plan, we fell in love with it. However, we learned that someone else was interested in purchasing it, so we were second in line. Needless to say, our hearts sank at the news.

But this was the Lord's plan for us, and we soon learned that the other buyer was not serious and that the apartment was ours if we wanted it. Because the owner wanted a quick sale, the asking price was only $30,000, an unheard of deal for a three-bedroom, 1100 square-foot apartment. However, our realtor thought we shouldn't buy it since the building's location was on the edge of a sketchy neighborhood known for its crime. After doing our own background checks, including a talk with a Norfolk policeman, we decided to buy the apartment.

By this time our airline tickets had been purchased, and take-off for Turkey was imminent. In lightning sequence our application to purchase the apartment was approved by the co-op board. Since it was owner-financed, we didn't need a bank loan. In record time, our house search was over; and with the assistance of friends, we moved from the beach house into the apartment. I never even slept one night in our new bedroom because my flight departed the next day. Since Dindy was leaving two weeks later, she took up residence alone amidst the moving boxes and clutter.

As we look back on this lesson in guidance, we are so grateful that God closed the door on the first property. Not only was it four times the cost, but it would have been more difficult to maintain from a distance. Because of the kindness of our neighbors, especially Tom and Dan, our apartment is well cared for while we're absent. Before returning to Turkey, we simply lock the doors with no cares for security or maintenance. Upon our return to Norfolk annually we are reminded of God's miracle each time we open the apartment door.

Cyndy Holter writes:

"Early in our marriage my husband Michael landed a good teaching job. He had been working at a popular steak house, and now it was time for him to use his gift of teaching. The school was located midway between several small towns requiring a long drive from our current home. However, the position afforded teachers the opportunity to live on campus in a mobile home park, which several others were doing. Moving a mobile home on site would give me and our one-year-old daughter more time with daddy and connect us with the community. We agreed this was best for our family.

Without hesitation we set out to find a mobile home. We prayed for the Lord to lead us and provide for us, since he promised to 'supply your every need, according to his riches in Christ Jesus' (Phil 4:19). After very little searching we came across a promising mobile home. Upon seeing it, we felt it was the one. The owner assured us she would hold it for twenty-four hours. Immediately we called the bank and Michael's father, so everything fell into place financially. I even began planning curtains and imagining our furnishings in this mobile home—*our* new home.

The next morning Michael was heading to work at the steak house. After asking me to call the owner back, he hesitated, 'We need to pray again.' He prayed, asking the Lord to close the door if this was not the right one for us. Of course, I prayed but not really. I was still imagining our new home and the joy of our move and his new job.

Off he went to work, and I called the owner. She didn't hesitate to tell me she had already sold it. I couldn't believe my ears! She had *promised* to hold it for us for twenty-four hours. She explained further that someone came up with the cash, and it was gone. In fact, the new owner knew us—a college pal named Doug. He too was starting his first teaching job. Crying, I called Michael to tell him the sad news. Confidently, he reminded me that we had asked the Lord to close the door. *He* had prayed that, but inside my mind and heart, I hadn't. Nevertheless, within a few weeks we found another mobile home and began our new adventure at the school.

A year later we ran into a college friend: to be exact, the sister of the man who bought 'our' mobile home. She asked if we knew what was going on with Doug. When Doug and his wife went to move 'our' mobile home, it broke in half en route. He was now facing a very involved lawsuit over the flawed mobile home. Needless to say, we were shocked, yet *so* grateful the Lord had protected us from disaster and legal complications.

As he promised, he had led us and provided just what we needed and when we needed it. This story has become a capstone reminder as we have sought God's face and will for our lives. When he says 'No' and closes the doors, we know we can trust him. He always knows what is best."

Reflection Questions

Describe the two closed doors that Paul and his companions received.

Looking at the map of the second journey, what things come to mind?

How does knowledge of the Roman road system help you understand these three verses?

Could guidance be Paul's meaning when he refers to "help given by the Spirit of Jesus Christ" (Phil 1:19)?

What closed doors has the Holy Spirit used to guide you?

LESSON 11

God uses visions and dreams to guide us.

⁹ During the night Paul had a vision of a man of Macedonia standing and begging him, "Come over to Macedonia and help us." ¹⁰ After Paul had seen the vision, we got ready at once to leave for Macedonia, concluding that God had called us to preach the gospel to them. ¹¹ From Troas we put out to sea and sailed straight for Samothrace, and the next day we went on to Neapolis. (16:9–11)

⁹ One night the Lord spoke to Paul in a vision: "Do not be afraid; keep on speaking, do not be silent. ¹⁰ For I am with you, and no one is going to attack and harm you, because I have many people in this city." ¹¹ So Paul stayed in Corinth for a year and a half, teaching them the word of God. (18:9–11)

Paul's Guidance

Twice during the second journey Paul was guided through a vision, with both occurring at crucial junctures in his ministry. After traveling one thousand miles from Syrian Antioch to Troas, the apostolic party had run out of land; only the Aegean Sea lay ahead. As they waited for further direction, one night Paul saw in a dream, or night vision, a Macedonian man inviting them to come over to Macedonia. How Paul was able to discern his geographical identity, we aren't told. Perhaps it was some characteristic piece of clothing or his accent. Macedonia was the Roman province now part of northern Greece (to distinguish it from the country of Macedonia).

Paul, Silas, and Timothy interpreted the vision to mean that they were to preach the gospel in Macedonia. The weeks of indecision, of not knowing their destination, were now over. Once this guidance was received, the three secured passage on a ship to Neapolis, an important Macedonian port situated on the trans-Balkan Roman road called the Via Egnatia. This passage marks an important geographical transition for the gospel: it now moves from the continent of Asia to the continent of Europe. It is also the first occurrence of a "we" passage in Acts in which the author now participates in the story. These "we" sections appear to be part of a travel diary composed by a travel companion, perhaps Luke himself.[1] The "we" author journeyed with the group as far as Philippi after a ten-mile walk inland from Neapolis. A well-preserved section of the Via Egnatia still exists west of Kavala.

Upon their arrival in this Roman colony it is ironic that that they don't meet a Macedonian man but rather a woman from the Lydian city of Thyatira (16:14). (Thyatira was one of the Seven Churches; Rev 2:18–29). The adversity experienced during the first journey recurs in Macedonia. Paul and Silas are wrongly jailed in Philippi after Paul cast a spirit of divination out of a slave girl. After their release the magistrates asked them to leave so they would no longer disturb their city (16:16–40).

The apostles continued to Thessalonica, the capital of the province. After initial success in the synagogue, some Jews who were jealous incited a riot against Paul and Silas. Again the charge was that these troublemakers were turning the world upside down. Jason and the other local believers were forced to post a bond to ensure that the apostles, who were proclaiming a king other than Caesar, would leave (17:1–9).

Under the cover of night they fled to Berea. The next day they went into the synagogue there and received a positive response to their message. But opponents from Thessalonica soon arrived to incite the Bereans against the apostles. Leaving Silas and Timothy behind, Paul departed to the coast with an escort of Bereans to catch a ship to Piraeus, the port of Athens (17:10–15).

Arriving in Athens, Paul must have had great expectations about seeing this center of civilization and philosophy. But he was to be disappointed: the agora, or civic marketplace, was full of statues and altars to various

---

1. For more on these sections see my review, "'We' Passages in Acts."

pagan gods and goddesses. Again he preached in the synagogue, but was also asked to address the civic leaders on the Areopagus, or Mars Hill. His message about the resurrected Jesus was mocked by almost everyone. Although not forcibly expelled, Paul must have felt some discouragement over the small spiritual harvest in this renowned city (17:16–34).

From Athens Paul made the 65-mile journey down the coast to Corinth, capital of the province of Achaia. Another Roman colony, another synagogue, another ministry opportunity: yet each new city seemed to bring more adversity. As Paul experienced initial success in the synagogue, he must have experienced *déjà vu*—the same tape playing, only a different time and a different place. After Silas and Timothy arrived from Macedonia, Paul devoted more time to preaching. Then opposition at the synagogue forced Paul to move next door to the house of Titius Justus (18:1–8). When was the other shoe to drop? What person or event would prompt his expulsion from Corinth?

In this context Paul received another night vision from the Lord with the encouraging words: "Don't be afraid!" Paul would recognize this as the same exhortation given to Abraham (Gen 15:1), Gideon (Judg 6:23), Daniel (Dan 10:12), and Mary (Luke 1:30). He was instructed to keep speaking about Jesus and not to be quiet. Like Isaac (Gen 26:24) and Jeremiah (Jer 15:20), the Lord promised Paul that he would be with him. Perhaps most meaningful was the Lord's reassurance that no one would attack and harm him. The physical and psychological abuse dealt by his opponents in city after city must have weighed heavily on Paul. The promise of a respite from this trauma must have been liberating. The Lord further assured Paul that he had many people in Corinth. This referred not only to those who had already become believers under Paul's ministry but also to those who would believe in Jesus through his future preaching.

The result of this assurance was almost two years of unhindered teaching of God's word in Corinth. This was the longest period that Paul had stayed in one place since ministering with Barnabas in Syrian Antioch. Luke does record a conflict with the Jewish leaders in Corinth that precipitated an appearance before the governor Gallio. However, Paul received no punishment; only the synagogue leader Sosthenes was beaten. Instead of being run out of town, Paul himself chose when to leave. He sailed with Priscilla and Aquila to Ephesus from Cenchrae, the eastern port of Corinth, where he got a haircut related to a personal vow (18:11–18).

Guidance Today

In the early morning hours of January 4, 2016, I had a dream: I was handing a copy of my book *Biblical Turkey* to John Bass, America's ambassador in Ankara. Such a dream was unusual for me since most of mine are nonsensical. So the next morning I told Dindy about it. Thinking I should act upon the dream, I immediately sent an email to the embassy asking for the ambassador's mailing address. However, I never received a reply, so was puzzled about the next step. Various projects and travel soon preoccupied me, so I largely forgot about the dream. But periodically I would think about it and ask the Lord to make a way if he intended that I get my book to the ambassador.

In the middle of March I received an email from the embassy stating that its representatives were going to hold a consular meeting for American citizens in Antalya. I signed up to attend and noted it in my calendar. Several days before the meeting the Holy Spirit reminded me of the dream and put the thought in my mind that this was the way to get the book to Ambassador Bass. After the March 24 meeting, I introduced myself to the embassy representative and presented him with a copy of my book. I also asked him if he would deliver a copy to the ambassador. Taped to the book was my business card with a brief, handwritten note extending best wishes to Mr. Bass.

When I handed the books to the representative, I never told him about the dream. It's not that I was embarrassed, but there was no reason to introduce potential spiritual misunderstanding into an innocuous act of gift-giving. Fast forward to the evening of June 21, 2017. I was in the American ambassador's residence in Ankara for the annual dinner of the Friends of the American Research Institute in Turkey (FARIT), of which I am a member. The ambassador was absent, so his wife Holly was hosting the dinner. In the dessert line I introduced myself to her and asked if they had received the copy of *Biblical Turkey* that I had sent. She acknowledged its reception, thanked me for it, and said it had been useful in their explorations of Turkey. From the moment of my dream, my initial attempt to send the book, its delivery to an embassy representative, and my conversation with the ambassador's wife, almost a year and a half had passed. Again it demonstrated to me that divine guidance requires patience to see its outworking.

"John" writes:

"God had called us to prepare to serve as Bible translators in the Middle East. We were amazed to see how one door after another was opened up for us. However, as we got close to going, some problems arose, and we weren't sure if God was showing us that he didn't want us to go to that particular country. During this time of uncertainty, on Sunday at church, our pastor invited us to the front, and we described our situation to everyone in the congregation. After the service a woman came up to us and said that God had given her a vision while we were speaking. Since God didn't usually give her visions, she was affected especially by what God had shown her. She described how she had seen my wife and me bringing a Bible to the people group in the Middle East that we were planning to go and serve. We felt like this was a clear sign from God that we were in fact supposed to be going! And over the years that same vision has encouraged us during other times of uncertainty."

"Bahar" writes:

"I was in my mid 50s at that time and had suffered from epilepsy for over twenty years. One night I had a dream or vision. Whether I was awake or sleeping, I'm not sure. I saw the ceiling above me beginning to open. Suddenly a bright light entered my room becoming brighter and brighter. I then saw a hand coming down that hovered over my body without touching me. Dark smoke began to come out of my hands and fingers. After the hand was withdrawn, I saw its owner—a man in bright white. He next put his hand on my head, and I could feel it. The man then said in an inaudible but understandable voice, 'I am healing you, and you will be healed for the rest of your life. You will be healed. Go to the light.' He repeated 'Go to the light' several times.

I was wondering what the man in white meant by 'light.' Since he used the word 'ışık' for light and not the Islamic word 'nur,' I knew I wasn't supposed to go to the mosque. I did some research on the Internet using the search word 'ışık' (light) and found the Işık (Lighthouse) Church in Izmir, which I then contacted. I wasn't yet ready to go to a church, so began to communicate by phone and email with several believers there for a few months. I also received some books which helped me to understand the Christian faith. I knew somehow that the man in the vision or dream was

Jesus. Later when I read the verse about Jesus being the light (ışık in Turkish) of the world in John 8:12 and 9:5, I understood.

In the meantime I went to the doctor and had various tests done. The doctor didn't believe the results and sent me to a different clinic with newer MRI machines. These also confirmed my healing. Finally, I decided to come to the Işık Church and began to attend the Alpha course. Soon I gave my life to Jesus and was baptized. When I gave my testimony, I brought all of my medical records showing my condition before and after the healing. I remain healed today nine years later and take no medication.

After my healing I was afraid to tell my son, who was in the military at the time. When he came home, I invited two leaders from the church to be with me when I told my son about my encounter with Jesus. This was the first time that these Christian friends had ever been in my home. My son listened carefully to my story; and instead of getting angry, he was very touched. He started to come to church with me, and we also began to attend the Alpha course together. I began to host a weekly discipleship meeting in our home. My son began to write love songs to Jesus and play them on his guitar. He still loves Jesus, and I hope he continues walking in the light of Jesus."[2]

Reflection Questions

How was the Troas vision pivotal for guiding Paul on the next stage of his journey?

Do you think Paul expected adversity after the vision summoned them to Macedonia?

Why were Athens and Corinth important cities for Paul?

How did the vision that Paul received in Corinth have significance for his ministry there?

Have you ever received a dream or vision that provided guidance for your life? If so, describe it.

2. Pseudonyms are used to protect the privacy of "John" and "Bahar." Dindy and I attended the Lighthouse Church in Izmir for six years and became acquainted with "Bahar" and her extraordinary story. My thanks go to Lighthouse leaders Matt Black and especially Judith Frank who transcribed her account.

5

The Third Journey

LESSON 12

God uses open doors to guide us.

[19] They arrived at Ephesus, where Paul left Priscilla and Aquila. He himself went into the synagogue and reasoned with the Jews. [20] When they asked him to spend more time with them, he declined. [21] But as he left, he promised, "I will come back if it is God's will." Then he set sail from Ephesus. [22] When he landed at Caesarea, he went up to Jerusalem and greeted the church and then went down to Antioch. [23] After spending some time in Antioch, Paul set out from there and traveled from place to place throughout the region of Galatia and Phrygia, strengthening all the disciples . . .. [1] While Apollos was at Corinth, Paul took the road through the interior and arrived at Ephesus . . .. [8] Paul entered the synagogue and spoke boldly there for three months, arguing persuasively about the kingdom of God. (18:19–23; 19:1, 8)

Paul's Guidance

Paul finally arrived in Ephesus over two years after being diverted northward at the beginning of his second journey. Despite ministry success in Macedonia and Achaia, Paul probably still wondered about the purpose of the prohibitions that brought him to Troas. Now he was in Ephesus, and by this time a fledgling Christian community already existed there. He was not its founding apostle as in Philippi, Thessalonica, Berea, and Corinth.

70

As was his custom, Paul went into the synagogue in Ephesus and presented his message about Jesus there. In Pisidian Antioch the leaders invited Paul and Barnabas to speak in the synagogue (13:15). And in Athens Paul used a similar open door to speak to the members of the Areopagus (17:19). However, despite the favorable welcome in Ephesus, Paul declined the invitation to spend more time in the synagogue.

What was behind his surprising decision? First, Paul had been traveling for almost three years and knew that the church in Antioch was probably wondering what had happened to him. So he wished to report the results of his church-planting efforts. Second, he had been tasked with circulating the letter about the council's decision so he wanted to report to the apostles the response of the Gentile believers. Third, Paul usually visited Jerusalem during one of the three Jewish festivals, so he wanted to worship at the temple. A fourth reason perhaps was to discover what had happened to Barnabas and John Mark after their separation and to learn the outcome of their journey. So Paul left Ephesus and sailed to Caesarea, the port of Judea, and went up to Jerusalem. Missing in the Greek text are the words "to Jerusalem," but translators rightly supply it because of a parallel construction in 15:2 and 21:12 where Jerusalem is explicitly mentioned.

Greeting the church there was more than just "hi and bye." It involved meetings, reports, prayer, and reconfirmation of mission. After a successful time with the apostles and the Jerusalem church, Paul made the long journey to Syrian Antioch for an extended time of R & R. Note that the return phase of the second journey is summarized in just two verses. The distance covered in 18:21–22 was approximately 1160 miles and took a minimum of forty days to travel by sea and land.[1]

For his third journey Paul was no doubt commissioned again by the church in Antioch. He knew where he was going, for an open door awaited him in Ephesus. This is a significant observation about how open doors guided Paul: he did not need to go through them immediately. Since the door was truly open, it would be open for him later as well. Understanding this principle, Paul took care of outstanding business before returning to Ephesus to go through that open door. Along the way he revisited the churches in Galatia, now for the fourth time. He must have been encouraged to see their progress in Christian discipleship since he had first preached there. Again the journey of 725 miles from Syrian Antioch to

---

1. A web site useful for calculating travel time and distance is: http://orbis.stanford.edu/.

Ephesus is described in just two verses (18:23; 19:1). The open door in Ephesus proved to be a significant one. Paul ministered in the city for almost three years with notable success. Opposition organized by Demetrius and the silversmiths eventually closed the door on Paul's time in Ephesus (see Lesson 13).

Another situation involving an open door soon presented itself after Paul left Ephesus. He traveled up the coast to Troas where the vision of the Macedonian man was received on the second journey (16:8–10). Again something significant happened here linked to the subject of guidance. Writing from Macedonia shortly after, Paul told the Corinthians, "Now when I went to Troas to preach the gospel of Christ and found that the Lord had opened a door for me. . ." (2 Cor 2:12). If Paul used the open and closed door principles of guidance seen so far, we would assume that Paul walked through that open door. However, Paul did not stay in Troas for an extended time of ministry. Nevertheless, he remained long enough to win believers and start a church there (see Lesson 15).

Why didn't Paul go through the open door? His reason was: "I still had no peace of mind, because I did not find my brother Titus there. So I said goodbye to them and went on to Macedonia" (2 Cor 2:13). Because of his spiritual and emotional conflict regarding the Corinthians, Paul decided to continue traveling to find Titus. Paul had sent Titus to Corinth as his personal representative, and Paul was anxious to learn the response of the Corinthians. During his time in Ephesus Paul dealt with many problems related to the Corinthian believers. Acts 19 is silent about Paul's ongoing relations with the Corinthian church. However, this extensive involvement can be reconstructed from 1 and 2 Corinthians. Paul had evidently suggested to Titus that they meet in Macedonia or Troas, which points to an established travel network that existed in the early church.

Paul did eventually meet Titus in Macedonia, and his report greatly comforted Paul (2 Cor 7:6–7). This scenario also provides a possible answer to the question of why the Spirit diverted Paul from Ephesus and to Corinth on the second journey. It was necessary for Paul to be in close proximity to Corinth so during his three years in Ephesus he could receive representatives and letters from the Corinthian church and travel there himself once. Consequently, Paul's geographical situation was ideal for dealing with the issues in the church that arose after he left Corinth.

Guidance Today

One day in 2015 an Australian scholar named Tim Foster showed up at the St. Paul Cultural Center in Antalya. Tim is the vice principal of Ridley College in Melbourne and had visited Turkey a number of times on personal and group trips. He was interested in starting a program that would bring Ridley students to Antalya for a residential program that would provide cross-cultural, biblical, and archaeological experiences. Tim asked if I would be interested in becoming the academic liaison for the program. Needless to say, I was very interested in this proposal. I had been teaching online courses for years, and was attracted to the idea of teaching students face-to-face again. Tim developed a partnership proposal with the first group of students scheduled to come in May 2016. What a tremendous open door, I thought! As Dindy and I thought and prayed about the possibility, the more excited we became.

Over the following months Tim and I discussed the courses to be taught. For two years I had been trying to organize an epigraphy seminar in Antalya. There is a great need for New Testament scholars and graduate students to know more about Greek and Latin inscriptions and how to use them in their scholarship. However, no one was sponsoring such a seminar. I had contacted an epigrapher named Rosalinde Kearsley, who taught at Macquarie University in Sydney. Ros agreed to lead the seminar. However, we could never get enough people to enroll to make it feasible financially. Ros had a small group from her home church, St. Paul's Castle Hill, who wanted to come including her pastor John Gray and his wife. I proposed to Tim that this be one of the courses offered to the Ridley students. Ros would teach in the morning, and I would lead afternoon field studies to local biblical sites. At last, the critical number was reached to conduct the seminar.

Tim also asked me to teach Revelation because of my academic work in that book. This seemed an additional open door for sharing my years of research with an interested group of students in the land of the Seven Churches. And the other amazing thing about the proposed program: I would be home every night to sleep in my own bed. Little did I know as Tim and I began our discussions for this Ridley program that Regent University would be terminating my position as visiting professor a few months later (see Lesson 14). Since God knew this, he was already opening another teaching opportunity so that the shock of the Regent termination was mitigated by the knowledge that I was soon to become an adjunct lecturer in

New Testament at Ridley College. In May-June 2016 eleven Ridley students studied in Antalya as part of the inaugural program. The next group for the Mediterranean study is scheduled for December 2017-January 2018, and Tim's hope is to conduct this program biennially, something I gladly welcome.

Marius Nel writes:

"As native South Africans, it has always been a dream of my wife Jampie and me to work and minister in Cape Town. In my case, it was specifically to obtain an academic position at the Theological Faculty of Stellenbosch University. In a period in which the multiracial transformation of South Africa's universities is a national priority, the latter seemed an impossibility. And the odds of my wife being called to pastor a church in the Cape seemed equally improbable since there are very few examples of female Dutch Reformed clergy being the sole minister in a congregation. At the time we had been co-pastoring a congregation in Pretoria for eighteen years.

In 2010 I had to attend a meeting at the faculty at Stellenbosch during which I heard 'by chance' that a position in New Testament was about to be advertised. During lunch at a nearby wine farm I told my wife that it would be wonderful if, against all the odds, I could get the position. And in the spirit of building dream castles, she could get then get a position in a congregation in Parow, 34 kilometers from Stellenbosch. The manse for the pastor there would provide our family with a place to stay. I mentioned Parow since it was an area in which congregations could not always afford a full-time minister. Six months later the position at the university was finally advertised, and I applied. However, there were no positions available for my wife in the Cape.

After another three months a friend told us about a congregation where a position was opening up. I decided to view the church on Google Earth to see where it was: Oostersee, a suburb right next to Parow. While viewing the church building on street viewer, my daughter, then seventeen, walked by my desk, and seeing the church remarked that she had seen it before. Since she had never been to Parow, my response was that she was mistaken. She, however, went to her room and returned with a CD cover of her favorite band—and indeed it had a photo of the church on the cover! Her conclusion was that we were on our way to the Cape.

God uses open doors to guide us.

After m y w ife a nd I h ad b een i nvited t o o ur r espective i nterviews, we had a long wait during which we heard nothing. Then one night my phone rang at 18:00. It was the dean at Stellenbosch offering me the position of teaching New Testament. My wife was away visiting congregants so I decided to wait till she returned to tell her the good news. Before she returned, our phone rang again. It was from the congregation she had applied for. Their vote on their vacant position resulted in a 12–12 vote after which they prayed and cast the lot. My wife was selected! Upon her return home she discovered that in two hours everything had changed; against all natural odds God had indeed called us to the Cape."

Reflection Questions

Why was the collaboration of Priscilla and Aquila important for Paul and his ministry?

How much time elapsed between the prohibition not to preach in Asia and Paul's arrival in Ephesus?

Why didn't Paul stay in Ephesus and preach in the synagogue after he was invited?

What was the purpose of Paul's visit to Jerusalem at this time?

Can you recall an open door that the Holy Spirit used to guide you?

LESSON 13

God uses Spirit-led decision making to guide us.

²¹ After all this had happened, Paul decided in the Spirit to go to Jerusalem, passing through Macedonia and Achaia. "After I have been there," he said, "I must visit Rome also." ²² He sent two of his helpers, Timothy and Erastus, to Macedonia, while he stayed in the province of Asia a little longer. (19:21–22)

Paul's Guidance

At the close of his time in Ephesus Paul began to pray about the next step in his ministry. Of all the cities visited during his journeys, Paul had now stayed the longest in Ephesus. His ministry success included performing extraordinary miracles (19:8–20). Fear had gripped the city after a demonized man beat up some Jewish exorcists who tried to cast out a demon in Paul's name. New believers burned their magic scrolls publicly. The effect was that both Jews and Gentiles, not only in Ephesus but throughout the province of Asia, heard the word of the Lord.

"Where next?" was his natural question. The Spirit now intervened to provide guidance in a fresh way. The translation, "decided in the Spirit," reflects the Greek text of 19:21 as well as the NIV footnote. Other possible translations of the verb *tithēmi* are "resolved" (NRSV, ESV) or "purposed" (NKJV).

God uses Spirit-led decision making to guide us.

What was the backstory for this Spirit-led decision? Writing a few months later to the Romans, Paul described his predicament: "But now that there is no more place for me to work in these regions" (Rom 15:23). At first glance Paul's comment seems impossible; surely there were still many unreached places to evangelize in the eastern Roman Empire. However, for Paul's church-planting strategy to succeed, he didn't need to visit physically every city. He left that to his converts like Epaphras who had come to faith in Ephesus and then took the gospel back to the Lycus River valley where he planted churches in Hierapolis, Laodicea, and Colossae (Col 1:7; 4:12–13).

Paul was now looking westward to Rome as the direction for fresh apostolic work and to see the Roman Christians "since I have been longing for many years to visit you" (Rom 15:23). The Greek noun *epipotheia*, translated "longing," is found only here in the New Testament. Paul's own "desire" (NKJV; NRSV) to visit Rome was motivating this decision in the Spirit.

Paul had encountered many Christians from Rome in his ministry travels. The extensive list of greetings in Romans 16 validates this observation. He labored and ministered extensively with Priscilla and Aquila, so he knew much about the church there despite having never visited it. Plus Rome was the political capital of the empire and the center of commerce and religion. Despite Rome's faults, and there were many, Paul must have had some patriotic feelings as a Roman citizen. So Paul's eagerness to visit the Roman believers was motivating his decision to visit Rome.

But Rome was only to be a stopping point for ministry in the Western Roman Empire: "I plan to do so when I go to Spain. I hope to see you while passing through and to have you assist me on my journey there, after I have enjoyed your company for a while" (Rom 15:24). Whether a visit to Spain was already in Paul's mind while in Ephesus, we don't know. For Luke tells us only that Rome was a destination. However, at some point Paul developed a plan to preach the gospel in Spain. Hispania, the Roman name for Iberia, consisted of three provinces: Baetica, Lusitania, and Tarraconesis. Twenty-two Roman colonies had been founded by Augustus in Hispania.

Depending on the time of year, travel by land along Roman roads through northern Italy and southern Gaul took at least fifty days over a distance of almost 900 miles. A direct sea journey from Ostia, the port of Rome, to Tarraco, the capital of the province Tarraconesis, took eight days of some 615 miles. So Paul was considering a significant commitment of time and resources in formulating this strategy.

A further interesting detail must be noted. While the eastern Roman Empire was Greek-speaking, the western part was Latin-speaking. Fluent in Hebrew, Aramaic, and Greek, Paul was well-equipped to preach to any audience in the East. As a Roman citizen he undoubtedly had a rudimentary knowledge of Latin, which had undoubtedly improved during his visits to Roman colonies like Pisidian Antioch, Philippi, and Corinth.

But to preach in a new language is a considerable achievement! Those of you who have tried know the challenge of communicating theological concepts in another language. This was especially true in the later first century when a Latin translation of the Old Testament didn't even exist. Individual Christians were just beginning to make such translations that came to be known as *Vetus Latina* (Old Latin). Yet we see the apostle confident to go to unreached cities in Spain to communicate the gospel to their Latin-speaking residents. This says a lot about Paul—his mental acumen and passion to preach the gospel to whomever, wherever.

But before Rome and Spain, another journey had to be undertaken first. As you consider Paul's decision making in the Spirit here, it is dizzying. Even today the geographic realities in these verses are vast. I have traveled to these destinations; and whether by land in cars or buses, by sea on ferries, or by air in jets, the distances are still exhausting. And Paul was doing this on foot or in wind-powered ships! His final destination was Jerusalem, but first he had to go in the opposite direction to Macedonia and Achaia and revisit the churches that he had started on the second journey.

While Luke does not tell us the reason for this leg of the journey, Paul does in his letter to the Romans: "Now, however, I am on my way to Jerusalem in the service of the Lord's people there. For Macedonia and Achaia were pleased to make a contribution for the poor among the Lord's people in Jerusalem" (Rom 15:25–26). The word for "contribution" in the Greek text is a familiar one: *koinōnia*. Paul expected the fellowship of the Gentile believers to be made tangible through their financial sharing. Shortly after leaving Troas and finding Titus somewhere in Macedonia, Paul wrote his second canonical letter to the Corinthians. In it he spoke extensively about this collection to prepare the Corinthians for his upcoming visit (2 Cor 8:1–9:15).

Part of Paul's decision making in the Spirit relates to his belief that the Gentile churches needed to support financially the needy in Jerusalem:

"Indeed they owe it to them. For if the Gentiles have shared in the Jews' spiritual blessings, they owe it to the Jews to be of service to them in material blessings" (Rom 15:27). The final clause of this verse has been changed to follow the ESV and NRSV translations. For it is from the Greek verb *leiturgeō*—"to perform a public service"—that we get the noun "liturgy." Paul saw the collection for the saints as a religious obligation that he must initiate.

This conviction was motivating his decision in the Spirit to go hundreds of miles out of his way to make this happen. He continued: "So after I have completed this task and have made sure that they have received this fruit, I will go to Spain and visit you on the way" (Rom 15:28). Whether the Spirit had assigned this task or Paul took it on himself as a scriptural mandate is unknown. However, as a man of the Spirit who grounded his decisions in prayer, Paul knew that this task was divinely directed. Making a circuitous detour was immaterial to him, as long as the decision he made in the Spirit in Ephesus was carried out.

Garry Friesen uses Paul's plan to go to Rome as a test case for decision making. He mentions Paul's decision in Acts but goes to the book of Romans to illustrate the specific stages of his decision.

1. Purposes: Paul's spiritual goals were based on God's moral will (Rom 1:11–13; 15:20)

2. Priorities: Not knowing how much time he had, he prioritized his goals (Rom 15:23–28)

3. Plans: He devised strategic plans to accomplish his purposes (Rom 1:13; 15:23–28)

4. Prayer: He prayerfully submitted himself and his plans to God's sovereign will (Rom 1:8–10)

5. Perseverance: When his plans were providentially hindered from being accomplished, he assumed the delay was God's will. Instead of being discouraged, he adjusted the timetable for these plans to be carried out (Rom 1:10, 13; 15:22–24).

6. Presentation: He based his decisions on God's moral will and his personal application of wisdom (Rom 1:8–13; 15:20–29).[1]

---

1. Used by permission of Garry Friesen. For a summary of Friesen's approach see his "Principles."

Friesen's model, although somewhat involved, shows from another perspective what is involved in making a decision in the Spirit.

Guidance Today

In August 1997 I moved to Tulsa, OK, to begin teaching at Oral Roberts University. In December of that year Dindy resigned her ministry position at Kempsville Presbyterian Church, and we sold our house in Virginia Beach to a long-time friend Denise Damoude. Dindy then joined me in the new house we had purchased in Tulsa. My teaching was going well at ORU; I greatly enjoyed the positive interaction with students and colleagues. However, Dindy had a very difficult time adjusting to our new environment. Unable to find any ministry positions at local churches, she was forced to work in other jobs that were unfulfilling. She lacked her usual joy and upbeat temperament, and as the saying goes, "When mama's not happy, nobody's happy." During my tenure at ORU I also led several student trips to Turkey plus did a personal research trip there.

One day Dindy suggested that we consider moving to Turkey since I spent so much time there. This suggestion was motivated in part by her desire to leave Tulsa. So we began to pray about that possibility. Around this time two negative experiences produced great internal conflict between me and the ORU administration (see Lesson 9). So in the spring of 2001 I resigned my teaching position, and we decided to travel around Turkey that fall. This would be our "spy out the land" trip to see if God was guiding us to relocate there. From September to December we were based in four different cities and sought counsel from friends about making the move.

On New Year's Eve 2001 Dindy and I were back in Virginia Beach staying at a waterfront hotel. It was snowing on the beach, a rare occurrence. We were debriefing about our time in Turkey and asking the Lord if the door was open to move there. Previously we had gone to the oceanfront to pray about major decisions and found that God often spoken to us in that tranquil beach setting. This time was no exception: we felt the Spirit encouraging us to proceed with plans to move to Turkey.

As mentioned in Lesson 7, there is sometimes a delay between receiving guidance from the Lord and the actual execution of that word. We felt strongly that we should return to the Hampton Roads area and reconnect with our home church because of its interest in Turkey and supportive environment. So we rented an apartment in Norfolk and moved our belongings from storage in Tulsa. Dindy got a job again at Kempsville Presbyterian Church.

However, this transition was difficult for me. I couldn't find any adjunct teaching positions initially, and my only employment was occasional editing and writing. Dindy carried the financial weight, while I continued to travel to Turkey as opportunity allowed. Early in 2004 we decided the time was right to relocate to Turkey. Miraculously, everything including financial support and the purchase of an apartment came together (see Lesson 10), and that spring we moved to Izmir. Our decision made in the Spirit several years earlier was at last being realized. An additional benefit was that each of us now felt fulfilled in our calling as we settled into life in Turkey.

Timothy George writes:

"I struggled to decide which seminary to attend. As a dyed-in-the-wool Southern Baptist preacher boy, everyone assumed I would choose one of our six denominational seminaries. My wife, Denise, and I visited one and met some of the professors. But after a long process of discernment, we decided to move to Boston, where I would attend Harvard Divinity School.

Countless people asked me, 'Why did you go to liberal Harvard?' Denise and I sensed that God was leading us there, but we had no infallible verification in advance. The decision was hard. While I earnestly prayed for direction, the counsel I received from others was decidedly mixed. Some friends thought I would likely lose my faith if I studied at such a school. (This had happened to others, so their concern was legitimate.) Others warned that I would forfeit all opportunities for ministry by leaving our cozy denominational cocoon. In this context, Hebrews 11:8–16 fastened itself to my mind and heart. The journey of Abraham and Sarah was made in response to a summons. The call came from outside them. Abraham and Sarah did not take a personality or spiritual gifts test and then decide to become pilgrims. They were summoned, and they knew it. We, too, knew we were summoned.

But a journey always involves displacement—and usually uncertainty. For Abraham and Sarah their journey was from *certainty to trust* and from *security to vulnerability*. During the seven years Denise and I spent in Boston—a thousand miles away from our home and families—we learned trust and vulnerability the hard way. I will never forget that empty feeling in my stomach when I came out of class one day to discover that my car had been stolen. Our house and the adjacent church building were broken into on five separate occasions, our few valuable items stolen. And the cultural difference was enormous: imagine trying to find grits in a Boston grocery store! But I had been summoned by the same God who called Abraham and Sarah as well as Paul to pick up stakes and set out into the unknown, and his promises cannot fail.

After completing my studies at Harvard, I joined the faculty of the Southern Baptist Theological Seminary in Louisville. Our time there was among the best in our lives. I loved teaching and had hundreds of wonderful students. Denise's own writing career began to flourish. And one of the benefits of teaching at Southern is the privilege of being buried in the nearby Cave Hill Cemetery. I loved walking through the cemetery and often took my students there on 'field trips' to stand near the resting places of the seminary founders and other saints. I even chose the plot where I hoped to be buried.

Then, one day, I received an unexpected call from the president of Samford University, Tom Corts. He said, 'We are thinking about starting a new divinity school here in Alabama, and we want to talk with you about becoming its founding dean.' I was taken aback. I had never been a dean, and had never wanted to be one. I was a scholar and a teacher. Seminary administration was the last thing that either I or those close to me thought that I would do. But Corts was persuasive, and I agreed to an interview. I met the school's benefactor, Ralph Waldo Beeson, and was impressed with his vision for theological education.

Faced with the decision, I consulted friends and again got mixed advice. I prayed and decided to spend an entire day at Cave Hill. I walked among the grave markers I had come to know so well. Some were elaborate monuments memorializing those who had done daring deeds of faith. But one of my favorite markers was that of the great New Testament scholar A. T. Robertson. His has a single verse inscribed on it: 'To me, to live is Christ and to die is gain' (Phil. 1:21). Hebrews 11:4 says of Abel that 'through his faith, though he died, he still speaks' (ESV). There was a kind of communion of saints in the cemetery that day, and I knew I had come there by special appointment.

From early morning until sundown, I walked, prayed, and read two Bible passages over and again. The first was Psalm 119. In repetitive stanzas, like waves breaking against the shore, the psalmist extols the Word of God. This psalm is a paean to the righteous ordinances of the Lord, to his testimonies, statutes, precepts, promises, and commandments. God's law, we are told, is an expression of his steadfast love and faithfulness. That day in the cemetery, my sense of vocation was confirmed as I allowed this psalm to shape me.

I also read and recited once again the story of Abraham and Sarah. When they were called by God, they obeyed, not knowing where they were going, not having received the things promised, but seeing them from afar and trusting that God would lead them at last to that city with foundations whose builder and maker is God (Heb. 11:10).

As I drove from Louisville to Birmingham to begin the work of Beeson Divinity School on June 1, 1988, I cannot say I was free from twinges of doubt. But I was sure of two realities: that God's Word will stand forever, for his promises cannot fail, and that I had once again been summoned by the same God who called Abraham, Sarah, and Paul to pick up stakes and set out into the unknown."[2]

Reflection Questions

How would you describe the concept of "deciding in the Spirit?"

At what stage in his travels was Paul making decisions about future ministry?

What is interesting about the geographical destinations related to Paul's decision?

Why do you think Paul wanted to visit Rome?

How would you involve the Holy Spirit in making important life decisions?

2. Used with permission and edited from George's article, "My Own Pilgrim's Progress."

LESSON 14

God uses changed circumstances to guide us.

[1] When the uproar had ended, Paul sent for the disciples and, after encouraging them, said goodbye and set out for Macedonia. [2] He traveled through that area, speaking many words of encouragement to the people, and finally arrived in Greece, [3] where he stayed three months. Because some Jews had plotted against him just as he was about to sail for Syria, he decided to go back through Macedonia. (20:1–3)

Paul's Guidance

Throughout Acts we have seen Paul repeatedly being forced to change his ministry plans and move on from various cities because of opposition. Two examples of Paul adjusting to changed circumstances are found at the beginning of Acts 20. An uproar instigated by Demetrius and the silversmiths climaxed in a tumultuous riot in Ephesus. Over 20,000 people gathered in the theater and shouted for two hours, "Great is Artemis of the Ephesians" (19:23–41). This occurred just after Paul had decided in the Spirit to revisit the churches in Macedonia and Achaia (see 1 Cor 16:5). Paul had already made the decision to leave; the riot apparently accelerated his timetable for departure.

The latter portion of his ministry in Ephesus was filled with challenges. In 1 Corinthians he wrote: "I face death every day—yes, just as surely as I boast about you in Christ Jesus our Lord. If I fought wild beasts in Ephesus with no more than human hopes, what have I gained?" (1 Cor 15:31–32; cf. 16:9). The wild beasts were Paul's enemies in the city who were conspiring to kill him. Each morning when he went to work with Priscilla and Aquila in the commercial agora or taught in the hall of Tyrannus, Paul didn't know if he would return home alive that night.

He further described the pressures of this period in 2 Corinthians written later in Macedonia: "We do not want you to be uninformed, brothers and sisters, about the troubles we experienced in the province of Asia. We were under great pressure, far beyond our ability to endure, so that we despaired of life itself. Indeed, we felt we had received the sentence of death. But this happened that we might not rely on ourselves but on God, who raises the dead" (2 Cor 1:8–9). So the riot proved to be the proverbial final straw. Paul had friends in high places in Ephesus—provincial officials called Asiarchs—and they strongly urged him not to appear in the theater. For they knew that his enemies would surely kill him there. After the riot ended, Paul gathered the disciples and gave them a brief word of encouragement. Saying goodbye, he traveled northward along the Roman road through Smyrna that followed the Aegean coast to Troas (2 Cor 2:12).

To the Corinthians Paul had previously communicated his plan to visit them on the way to Macedonia. However, the deteriorating situation in Ephesus forced him to alter it. Some Corinthians thought this change suggested vacillation on Paul's part. So Paul had to defend this decision to his opponents who were questioning his apostleship: "I planned to visit you on my way to Macedonia and to come back to you from Macedonia, and then to have you send me on my way to Judea. Was I fickle when I intended to do this? Or do I make my plans in a worldly manner so that in the same breath I say, 'Yes, yes' and 'No, no'?" (2 Cor 1:16–17). Perhaps Paul learned a lesson in guidance from this misunderstanding that he should be more tentative in announcing future plans (cf. James 4: 13–15). As the Scottish poet Robert Burns observed in his poem "To a Mouse": "The best-laid plans of mice and men often go awry."

Paul finally arrived in Greece, and during his three months in Corinth he wrote the book of Romans (Rom 16:23–24). Phoebe, a deacon at Cenchrea, was apparently the courier for the letter (Rom 16:1). As we saw in the previous lesson, at the conclusion of his letter to the Romans, Paul revealed his future travel plans projecting a visit to Rome on his way to Spain. But first he had to take the collection from the Gentile churches to Jerusalem.

Just as he was about to set sail from Cenchrea for the eastern Mediterranean coast of Syria, Paul received word of a plot against his life. Sailing was always the easiest way to travel in antiquity, especially with the northwest prevailing winds that would have brought Paul quickly to the port of Caesarea and then Jerusalem. It is possible that Paul was booking passage on a pilgrim ship chartered by Jews to bring them from Achaia to Jerusalem for the Feast of Passover. If Paul had boarded the ship, his enemies could have quickly dispatched him since there was no way of escape. Paul apparently had friends in Corinth's Jewish community who learned of the conspiracy and informed him of the danger. That Paul had previously been saved from a similar Jewish plot in Damascus (9:23–34) and would again be delivered from a future plot in Jerusalem (23:14–16) points to God's protective hand on his life.

With a sea journey out of the question, Paul was forced to backtrack through Macedonia, revisiting the churches there. On the inbound portion of the trip Paul had presumably told them of his plan to visit Jerusalem. So the believers were undoubtedly surprised when he showed up again. Accompanying him were representatives of various Gentile churches who now shared the burden of carrying and protecting the collection for the Jerusalem church. Representatives of Diaspora Jewish communities similarly carried large sums of money annually to Jerusalem for payment of the half-shekel temple tax required for every Jewish male over the age of twenty. In contrast, Paul's collection was a one-time offering to needy believers there whom he considered to be God's spiritual temple (1 Cor 3:16–17, 19; 2 Cor 6:16).

Once again we see Paul forced to modify his plans. Instead of celebrating the Feast of Unleavened Bread in Jerusalem, he now did it in Philippi (20:6). Nevertheless, he still hoped to arrive in Jerusalem for the Day of Pentecost (20:16). Paul's adaptability to changed circumstances is remarkable, with his flexibility ensuring ministry success as he was led by the Spirit.

Guidance Today

In 2004 my revised doctoral thesis was accepted by an academic publisher, and I had signed a contract for its publication. The publisher required me to format the text according to their editorial guidelines so it was camera-ready for printing. After many hours of preparing the manuscript, I was preparing to submit the file. Then disaster struck, or at least I thought so at the time. Suddenly a negative review from another scholar came in that was unfair and unsubstantiated, in my view. Despite the positive reviews of the other reviewers, the publisher decided to drop the project. Needless to say, I was devastated and upset over this abrupt termination of the contract. Days of editorial work were lost, and the book remained unpublished.

As I prayed about other options, another academic publisher was suggested to me. So I contacted Wipf and Stock about them possibly publishing the manuscript. Their initial response was positive so I prepared a sample chapter, revising it for their different style guidelines. The proposal was accepted, and the book was published finally in 2005.[1] After I began to teach Revelation at Regent University, I assigned that volume as a required textbook. The hardbound edition by the original publisher would have been too expensive for students to purchase. However, Wipf and Stock's edition was significantly less expensive and therefore affordable for classroom use. So the circumstance of changing publishers actually worked out both for my good and the good of my students.

In May 2015 I received an email from the interim dean of the School of Divinity at Regent University. He informed me that my position as a visiting professor had been terminated (I still serve as an adjunct professor). My termination was not unique; other visiting professors had similarly been released. This was quite a shock because I had been associated with Regent as a student and professor for over three decades. My decade of part-time teaching at Regent had been a godsend. Through the wonder of internet technology I was able to teach online courses from Turkey, conducting live lectures to students around the world using the Blackboard platform. Each spring I also organized and led a study tour for Regent students to one of the Bible lands in the eastern Mediterranean. Then in the fall while in the U.S., I often taught a residential modular course. So this half-time position was perfect since it provided the extra income necessary to live in Turkey. Now that income would be gone, or so I thought.

Earlier in 2015 I had been in contact with our financial advisor, Bob O'Brien (see Lesson 6). In November 2015 I was set to hit the magic retirement number—66. So my question to Bob was: Should I take retirement now or wait until age 70? We ran the numbers and saw there was no financial advantage to delay taking Social Security. So I filed for Social Security when I became eligible. A small severance from Regent plus additional income from advising a doctoral student assured my Regent paycheck through September. Then in November I qualified for my first retirement check. So the break in income lasted only one month. When I checked the amount that

1. Wilson, *Victor Sayings.*

Social Security was now depositing into my bank account, I was amazed to discover that the figure almost matched my previous income from Regent! Despite the changed circumstance that at first looked worrying, God was faithful to provide for our needs once again.

This year I have been reminded that changed circumstances are not always welcome. On the morning of February 9, 2016, I checked my email and found a message from our youngest son David. He, his wife Heather, and their four children (that is, four of our eight grandchildren) have lived in Istanbul for the past decade. To have them in the same country, only an hour away by plane, has been a great joy and blessing. While passing through Istanbul for a tour, I often made a stopover with them. Or when there was a cheap airfare Dindy and I made a quick weekend visit.

Last October David and Heather informed us that their project in Turkey was winding down. This and other factors were causing them to rethink their work and living situation here. We discussed the possibility of their return to the U.S. in the fall of 2018 when the project ended. We understood and supported them in this decision, although we were already saddened to think of their upcoming absence from Turkey.

Then came this email informing us that their timetable for relocation was moved forward by over a year. Wow! This news was like a punch in the stomach to me. Dindy was asleep, but I woke her to share it. We talked for a couple of hours about this changed circumstance and all it would mean. Again we supported David and Heather's decision but grieved over its implications. For example, our grandson Nathan loves pizza so we often planned our visits for Friday pizza night; soon such pizza nights would be over. Separated so far from the rest of our loved ones, it was a consolation to have at least some family in country.

Dindy and I will live through this changed situation. As many parents know, especially those with grandchildren, life comes in seasons. And this season of having our son and his family near us has ended. Nevertheless, the pain of this loss has been real, forcing us again to trust that God will lead us through life's changing circumstances. But we also rejoice knowing that God is faithful to lead our family as well!

Bill Cash writes:

"We do a bit of sailing, and I thought my serious fall from a roof in 2010 was the end of that. But God had other plans. Then Hurricane Sandy came ashore the New Jersey coast. We live at ground zero and lost both of our cars to the flood and received much water damage to our house. To offset our financial loss, we tried to sell the sailboat but were prevented from doing so. Somehow, like the birds of the air, all our needs were met.

In the spring of 2016 I begin to make plans for an extended sail when our daughter needed the help of my wife Katherine with her new and first baby. Katherine finished her grandmotherly duties in early June, and after a week or so of rest for her, we began making plans to cast off on the high tide of June 11 or 12. However, on June 10, while walking out the front door, I twisted my ankle and broke a bone in my left foot. Because of my frozen left elbow, a holdover of my earlier fall, I cannot use crutches. The orthopedic doctor put me in a walking boot and told me that it would take six weeks to heal. I set my sights on a new cast-off date.

Although my ankle started to heal quickly, I failed to wear the boot prescribed by the doctor and progress began to regress. So I got serious about wearing the boot and began to make sailing plans again. However, on July 26 my sister called with news that my dad had experienced a massive stroke. All morning long I was thinking: 'OK, my foot has kept me home; if my foot had healed on time I would have been out to sea. It could have taken me days to get back to help Mom and Dad if I had sailed.' Seven weeks after the break the doctor gave a positive prognosis, so I again began to set a date to cast off. Then Katherine got a call from our daughter that our grandson was sick, and she needed Katherine's help for a week because of some important meetings.

I was thinking to myself: 'Wow, are we ever going to start this trip? But then if my foot wasn't broken, we wouldn't have been here for Dad and now for Jenn as well, so the break in my foot is starting to look like a good thing.' The next visit with the doctor went well, and in my mind's eye I could see the Friday high tide with Katherine and me sailing out the cut on a two-week trip. But then I had got word that Dad's recovery was amazing and that he was being discharged to come home. However, I needed to help Mom and Dad during their first week at home.

By this time, I'd been working hard to have a good attitude. During my final visit to the doctor Katherine mentioned to him the pain in my calf. After examining it, he immediately ordered an ultrasound to test for a clot. After the test the ultrasound technician announced: 'I'm sorry to have to tell you but you do have a clot. And it's a big one: from your groin to your knee is all clot. I need to take you to emergency room right now.' The date?

8/9/16. Exactly six years from the fall that almost killed me. While lying on the table, having a quiet conversation in my head, I asked, 'Now what? Would I ever sail again?'

Because I had a left-over filter from the clot in my leg in 2010, the ER doctor gave me some blood thinner pills and sent me home. I soon learned from my present doctor that this was really a mistake since my old filter was now quite useless and should have been removed years ago. No one said much about how ugly this could have turned out. I don't normally go around trying to ascribe meaning to every little thing, but this chain of seemingly unrelated events, lining up for 'the good' is hard to overlook. Especially the date. One nurse said, 'With your bad luck you should just stay in bed.' I told her that I must have very good luck since I'm still alive. I neglected to mention I don't believe in luck at all. The inability to make my sailing trip undoubtedly saved my life."

Reflection Questions

What role did the riot in the theater play in Paul's departure from Ephesus?

What churches would Paul have visited after he left Ephesus?

Although unstated in Acts, why was it important for Paul to reach Corinth?

What was the changed situation that forced Paul to take the land route back through Macedonia?

Can you recall a changed situation that forced you to adjust your plans?

LESSON 15

God uses the compulsion of the Spirit to guide us.

[13] We went on ahead to the ship and sailed for Assos, where we were going to take Paul aboard. He had made this arrangement because he was going there on foot. [14] When he met us at Assos, we took him aboard and went on to Mitylene. . . .[22] "And now, compelled by the Spirit, I am going to Jerusalem, not knowing what will happen to me there. [23] I only know that in every city the Holy Spirit warns me that prison and hardships are facing me. [24] However, I consider my life worth nothing to me; my only aim is to finish the race and complete the task the Lord Jesus has given me—the task of testifying to the good news of God's grace. [25] "Now I know that none of you among whom I have gone about preaching the kingdom will ever see me again. (20:13–14, 22–25)

Paul's Guidance

Paul was at a critical phase in his public ministry at the end of the third journey. Traveling with a group of eight companions including the author of this extended "we" passage, he was carrying the collection from the Gentile believers to the church in Jerusalem. Once again Paul passed through Troas after departing from Philippi, where he had celebrated Passover. At the end of his weeklong stay in Troas, Paul met with a group of believers gathered to hear him one last time. As he preached through the night, the oxygen became thin because of the olive-oil lamps, and a listener named

Eutychus perched himself on a window ledge to get some fresh air. However, he dozed off and fell to his death three floors below. Interrupting his message, Paul rushed downstairs and raised Eutychus from the dead. Eutychus means "good luck," and indeed he was fortunate to have Paul there to bring him back to life! From Troas Paul made a solitary walk, unexplained by Luke, to Assos where he rejoined the coasting vessel that was carrying his companions (20:7–12).[1] The group sailed southward through the Aegean islands of Lesbos, Chios, and Samos, bypassing Ephesus.[2]

Arriving at Miletus, Paul summoned the Ephesian elders and delivered a farewell address to them (20:18–35).[3] In it he declared: "And now I am bound by the Spirit to go to Jerusalem" (20:22; NLT). The Greek verb *deō*—also translated "compelled" (NIV), "constrained" (ESV), and "captive" (NRSV)—is an important catchword in these later chapters. In 21:11 the prophet Agabus bound his own hands and feet with Paul's belt, declaring, "The Holy Spirit says, 'In this way the Jewish leaders in Jerusalem will *bind* the owner of this belt and will hand him over to the Gentiles.'" This combination of prophetic act and prophetic word confirmed what the Holy Spirit had been speaking to Paul throughout the journey "that prison and hardships are facing me" (20:23). Nevertheless, after Agabus' warning, the apostle reiterated his determination to continue: "I am ready not only to be *bound*, but also to die in Jerusalem" (21:13). This illustrates the Spirit's compulsion in Paul's decision making: nothing would deter him from the goal.

In Jerusalem Paul soon found himself in trouble with a crowd at the temple. The Roman commander arrested him and had him "*bound* with two chains" (21:33). In his speech before the crowd Paul noted the irony of his situation. Over two decades earlier he had traveled to Damascus to "*bind*" believers and bring them back to Jerusalem for punishment (22:5). Now he was the one bound in chains. When Paul was being interviewed by the Roman commander, he realized that Roman law had been violated because he had "*bound*" a Roman citizen (22:29). Paul was later back in Caesarea but this time "*bound*" as a prisoner of the Roman governor Festus (24:27).[4]

1. For more about this walk, see Thompson and Wilson, "Paul's Walk to Assos." In May 2017 Dindy and I along with Glen and Beth Thompson replicated this 31-mile walk with a group of friends and students.

2. For more about this sea journey, see my article, "Lukan Periplus."

3. For more on their coming to Miletus, see my article, "Ephesian Elders."

4. The NIV does not translate *deō* as "bind" in these verses, thus the verbal emphasis is lost. Other English translations usually give a more literal translation.

Somewhere along his journey, perhaps on his solitary walk to Assos, Paul had submitted himself to God's will for whatever lay ahead. Thus he was compelled by the Spirit long before anyone had bound him physically in Jerusalem and Caesarea. Paul's submission to the will of God is reminiscent of his Lord's submission to God's will in the Garden of Gethsemane. There Jesus prayed, "Father, if you are willing, take this cup from me; yet not my will, but yours be done" (Luke 22:42). After his betrayal Jesus was "*bound*" and brought to the chief priests, the Sanhedrin, and to Pilate (Mark 15:1; John 18:12–13). In conclusion, Paul's compulsion by the Spirit was critical because soon other voices would seek to dissuade him from taking up his own cup.

Guidance Today

In my younger days I played a lot of baseball and basketball, learning what competition was all about. Later I took up tennis and enjoyed the competitive nature of playing singles or doubles. While compulsions are often regarded as negative in the sense of addictions, they can also be positive. If we are compelled to do something with a worthy goal, a compulsion can be constructive. Without a compulsion to win, athletes would never have the discipline to train for years to win a gold medal in the Olympics. So too in the Christian life (1 Cor 9:24–27).

In 2004 my wife and I made the decision to move to Turkey (see Lesson 13). After a time of prayer and fasting, we felt that the Holy Spirit gave us the green light to relocate. However, as we began to share our plans with friends and family, this decision was met with skepticism, even fear, by some. In America's post 9/11 environment there was apprehension about what might happen to us in a Muslim country where Americans and Christians were presumed to be hated. While we thanked our loved ones for their concern, we felt compelled to follow the leading of the Holy Spirit regarding this relocation. Fortunately our local church was supportive of our move so their positive spiritual counsel was very critical for making our final decision.[5]

This decision has been tested through the years, most recently with the spate of terrorist incidents in Turkey in 2015–2016. The most recent travel warning of the U.S. State Department dated March 28, 2017, begins: "U.S. citizens are warned of increased threats from terrorist groups in Turkey.

5. This section is adapted from my devotional reflection, "Paul: Bound in the Spirit."

Carefully consider the need to travel to Turkey at this time, and avoid travel to southeast Turkey due to the persistent threat of terrorism." Such advisories certainly grab the attention of potential visitors, and the result has been the reduction of North American tourists to Turkey.

When our family and friends read such dire warnings, they naturally and frequently express their fears about our safety. While we understand their concern and ask them to pray for us, nonetheless, we continue to assure them that life in Antalya remains normal for us and that we are probably safer here than even in our apartment in Norfolk. However, we are not Pollyannaish in our assessment by refusing to look at reality. Events in Turkey during the summer of 2016 did cause us to reexamine our exit strategies and to do further emergency planning. Throughout, however, Dindy and I have felt God's compulsion to remain in the place where he has called us.

This is also related to our larger call to live in the Eastern Mediterranean, which is a troubled part of the world. I recently made a trip to Lebanon to visit Tyre and Sidon (see Lesson 16). Before going, I read the State Department's travel advisory dated February 15, 2017. U.S. citizens should "avoid travel to Lebanon because of the threats of terrorism, armed clashes, kidnapping, and outbreaks of violence, especially near Lebanon's borders with Syria and Israel." And Tyre is located only 25 miles from Israel's border.

Because of my research interests though, I must travel periodically to so-called "dangerous" places. But the Spirit has given me a rule of thumb to guide me regarding such travel. If I can locate a "person of peace" (Luke 10:6) to help facilitate my visit, I feel safe to go. God provided Athanasius for my research trip to Alexandria, Egypt, in March 2016 and Shadi for Lebanon in February 2017. There is peace and comfort knowing that the compulsion of the Spirit brought us to Turkey and that he continues to compel us to follow his call here and beyond.

M. Blaine Smith writes:

"The first major decision I faced as a very young Christian was remarkably easy. It concerned my involvement with a rock band I directed, the Newports. When I gave my life to Christ as a third-year college student, I was spending a lot of time managing and booking this group, which played frequently for local dances and social events. The question was whether or not God wanted me to continue performing with the group. At first it was easiest just to follow the course of least resistance, so I stayed in. But after several months the resistance on that path got much stronger. In fact, in an instant.

I was studying in a dormitory room at Georgetown University when suddenly it became crystal clear that God wanted me to leave the Newports. At least this was my perception. While I didn't hear an audible voice, I did have an overwhelming sense that God was prompting me. I must hasten to say that this was not a philosophical conclusion about music, such as "rock music is of the devil." I wasn't mature enough in the Lord to deal with an issue of that sort (and for the record, I don't believe that any form of music is moral or immoral in itself). The conviction was simply a deep, intuitive one. I was certain God was speaking to me and nudging me to quit this group.

I didn't question it. Within a day I spoke with practically everyone associated with the band—about ten people in all—and in the unsophisticated manner of a new Christian boldly asserted that God had spoken to me and told me to resign. Even though most of them questioned my lucidity, I had no doubt I had been led by God.

There is one factor, especially, which persuades me that this was an authentic experience of exceptional guidance and not just a grandiose delusion. Within about a week after making this decision, I simply stopped receiving phone calls from people wanting to hire the Newports. There was no clear explanation for this. The group's services had been in considerable demand up to this point, and most people wanting to hire the group wouldn't have known yet that I had quit. But for some reason the calls just quit coming in. I've never known how to explain this apart from its being a dramatic confirmation from the Lord that I made the right choice.

Of course, my interpretation of these events is subjective. There's no way ultimately to prove any explanation for them. Yet the evidence leads me to believe that I did have an experience of special guidance. The guidance to leave the Newports came at a time when I was very young in the faith and not ready to take responsibility for a major decision. God, I believe, was gracious to intervene and guide me in a direct manner. He even took care of the ramifications of that decision in a remarkable way."[6]

6. Smith, *Knowing God's Will*, 68–69, and used with permission.

Linford Stutzman writes:

"The vision to embark on the voyage of *SailingActs* came with remarkable clarity and force. As a professor at Eastern Mennonite University, I, along my wife Janet, was leading a group of twenty-six students for a semester-long study program in the Middle East. I was also beginning to look three years ahead to when I was due for my first sabbatical. I will never forget the day we were visiting the impressive first-century port of Caesarea, Israel. I was a stone's throw from the shore, standing on some of the ruins of the artificial harbor built by Herod the Great and thinking about how Paul had spent two years in prison there, awaiting transfer to Rome for his hearing with the Caesar. I wondered: 'How did he feel, heading toward Rome that day?' Then, as if hearing a voice from heaven on the road to Damascus, it hit me: 'There is only one way to find out.' And so the idea to buy an old sailboat in the Mediterranean and fix her up, then sail to all thirty-seven harbors visited by Paul mentioned in Acts was born.

I do not know exactly how to tell the difference between an impulsive powerful idea, and divine guidance, but this vision simply refused to die, or even fade. My wife, amazingly, was instantly supportive and ready to quit her job so we could explore the Mediterranean together. We began to act on the vision once we were back home in the USA by reading books, buying gear, searching for an old but affordable boat to purchase and fix up in the Mediterranean, taking sailing lessons in the Chesapeake Bay, and learning skills like navigation and knot-tying.

For the next two years we moved ahead toward the vision. We hung charts in our house and shared our plans with others, thus making it harder to back out. We read the stories of people who had left the security and predictability of home to follow God's call to the ends of the earth. I applied for the sailing sabbatical which was approved! Four months before the sabbatical was to begin, I finally I found a twenty-five-year-old Westerly 33 online that fit our limited budget. Six months later, after a brief inspection of the sadly neglected *Aldebaran* that was tied to the wharf of Volos, Greece, I shook hands with the Greek owner. Then it was unrelenting paperwork, fees, and bureaucracy followed by moving aboard and working twelve hours a day for six weeks, cleaning, repairing, outfitting, and finally changing the name from *Aldebaran* to *SailingActs*. The more time and effort we invested, the more our commitment grew. And it was this deep and growing commitment that kept us going through the waves of doubt and discouragement.

God uses the compulsion of the Spirit to guide us.

The long-anticipated launch finally came. It was June 17, 2004, 1:30 pm. I started the engine, loosened the ropes that had secured our boat to the wharf for three years, and with pounding hearts, *SailingActs* moved away from the security of the wharf. The vision given at Caesarea over three years earlier was happening! We were following Paul! For approximately ten minutes we celebrated. Then a squall hit us directly—high wind, slashing rain, thunder, lightning, and awful sea-sickness. We somehow made it through that trial and countless other new ones that seemed to occur on a daily basis for that first summer. Much later, in the cockpit aboard *Sailing Acts* firmly tethered at the time in the Ashkelon Marina in Israel, a guest spun the wheel and observed, 'You cannot steer a boat that is standing still.' So it is with guidance, it happens when moving forward.

It has been twelve years since we completed the routes of Paul, ending in Rome in July 2005. The decision to follow the strong vision in Caesarea has been one of the most significant and rewarding decisions that my wife and I have made since being married. We have been blessed in ways we did not imagine, most profoundly by sharing with countless others the experience of sailing the Mediterranean with Paul. However, we have not yet sold *SailingActs*, for we are not yet home."[7]

Reflection Questions

How would you describe the concept of being "compelled by the Spirit?"

How was Paul's walk from Troas to Assos related to his decision making?

What was the purpose and destination of the return leg of his third journey?

Why did the Holy Spirit begin to warn Paul about what lay ahead?

Can you give an example of feeling the Spirit's compulsion when making a decision?

7. For more on the Stutzmans' adventures, see www.emu.edu/sailingacts and Linford's book, *SailingActs*.

LESSON 16

God uses personal prophecy to guide us.

³ We landed at Tyre, where our ship was to unload its cargo.⁴ We sought out the disciples there and stayed with them seven days. Through the Spirit they urged Paul not to go on to Jerusalem. ⁵ When it was time to leave, we left and continued on our way. All of them, including wives and children, accompanied us out of the city, and there on the beach we knelt to pray. ⁶ After saying goodbye to each other, we went aboard the ship, and they returned home. ⁷ We continued our voyage from Tyre and landed at Ptolemais, where we greeted the brothers and sisters and stayed with them for a day. ⁸ Leaving the next day, we reached Caesarea and stayed at the house of Philip the evangelist, one of the Seven. ⁹ He had four unmarried daughters who prophesied. ¹⁰ After we had been there a number of days, a prophet named Agabus came down from Judea. ¹¹ Coming over to us, he took Paul's belt, tied his own hands and feet with it and said, "The Holy Spirit says, 'In this way the Jewish leaders in Jerusalem will bind the owner of this belt and will hand him over to the Gentiles.'" ¹² When we heard this, we and the people there pleaded with Paul not to go up to Jerusalem. ¹³ Then Paul answered, "Why are you weeping and breaking my heart? I am ready not only to be bound, but also to die in Jerusalem for the name of the Lord Jesus."¹⁴ When he would not be dissuaded, we gave up and said, "The Lord's will be done." ¹⁵ After this, we started on our way up to Jerusalem. (21:3–15)

Paul's Guidance

Because of the Holy Spirit's compulsion, Paul was now journeying to Jerusalem. Along the way, however, the Spirit suddenly began to give what seemed to be contradictory guidance. In his speech at Miletus, Paul mentioned the warnings that the Holy Spirit was giving about upcoming hardships and prison (20:23). How were such warnings being conveyed? They were apparently coming through personal prophecies delivered by believers in city after city. The prophecies possibly started in Philippi but certainly in Troas, which is perhaps why Paul made his solitary walk to Assos. Paul was not omniscient regarding his future. He thought his death in Jerusalem was likely, so he told the Ephesian elders that they should not expect to see him ever again. (Paul apparently did visit Ephesus again; 1 Tim 1:3). At his departure the elders wept, embraced, and kissed Paul, thinking this was the final goodbye to their beloved mentor and teacher (20:37–38).

At Patara Paul and his companions transferred to another vessel bound for the Phoenician coast of Syria (21:1–3). When their ship stopped in Tyre, Paul took the opportunity to call on the believers there. He had visited these churches previously during his journeys between Antioch and Jerusalem. Believers in Tyre with the gift of prophecy and prompted by the Spirit began to warn Paul of the dangers ahead. However, their human spirits seemingly got involved, and they framed their prophecies as warnings that Paul should cancel his plans to go to Jerusalem.[1] When the ship stopped in Ptolemais, Paul also met the believers there. We are not told what happened, but most probably a similar scene ensued: Paul was warned through personal prophecies not to continue to Jerusalem.

The next day Paul and his friends finally arrived at Caesarea. The deacon and evangelist Philip hosted him there, and his family included four daughters with the gift of prophecy. Although unstated, it is assumed again that these daughters through the Spirit also began to warn Paul about what lay ahead in Jerusalem. Whether they were mature enough to refrain from personal interpretations of their prophecies is unknown. News of Paul's arrival quickly made its way to Jerusalem. Whether Agabus went down to

---

1. In his writings Paul gives explicit instructions about how prophecy should function. The spirits of the prophets are under the control of each prophet because he or she can distinguish between praying, praising, and prophesying with the mind as opposed to doing that with the spirit/Spirit (1 Cor 14:13–15, 32). All prophecy must be judged by other believers, especially by other prophets (1 Cor 14:29; 1 Thess 5:19).

Caesarea based on this news or whether the Spirit prompted him to make the trip is unstated.

In Lesson 3 Agabus was introduced as the prophet who came from Jerusalem to Antioch and prophesied about a coming famine. In response to that prophecy Paul and Barnabas brought a donation from the believers in Antioch to those in Jerusalem. Whether Agabus' sudden appearance in Caesarea surprised Paul is not known. Yet he knew that Agabus was a proven and tested prophet who would speak accurately on behalf of the Lord.

Taking Paul's belt, Agabus bound his hands and feet with it. Speaking a personal prophecy (i.e., individual, not corporate as in Antioch), he declared through the Spirit that this is what the Jewish leaders would do to Paul in Jerusalem before handing him over to the Gentiles. As a mature prophet, Agabus did not put any "spin" on his prophetic declaration. It was the bystanders witnessing the binding and hearing the prophecy who now pleaded with Paul not to go up to Jerusalem. As we saw in Lesson 15, Paul had already been bound in the Spirit to complete the task. So these personal prophecies by believers, whose interpretation was well-meaning but misguided, did not prevent Paul from completing his mission. Agabus' prophecy simply confirmed the Spirit's compulsion received weeks before by Paul that reaching Jerusalem was the will of God. (See Appendix E: "Prophecy Today.")

Guidance Today

In December 1981 Dindy and I stood together on stage in the auditorium at Christ for the Nations in Dallas, Texas. It was the commissioning service for CFNI's winter graduates. I had dropped out of Hamline University in St. Paul, Minnesota, in 1968 to get involved in the anti-Vietnam War movement. After becoming a Christian in 1974 (see Lesson 1), I was not interested in further higher education and content with running my tree service and firewood business in Chadron, Nebraska. Our friends Jim and Stephanie Ansen had moved to Dallas to attend CFNI, and we visited them once. However, I remained disinterested in attending Bible school there. Besides, our pastor thought it unnecessary to go to school elsewhere for theological training, believing that everything needed for ministry preparation could be learned in the local church.

Dindy began to pray that I would soften my opposition, and finally in 1979 I agreed to enroll at CFNI, but just for one semester. We left most of our personal belongings in Nebraska since we planned to return, or at least I did. However, during a chapel service a life-changing incident occurred. I was seated in the balcony of that same auditorium listening to a guest speaker named Mario Murillo. While he was speaking, the Holy Spirit spoke to me clearly and called me to be a teacher of the Bible. The result of that calling was to abandon my plans to return permanently to Nebraska and to decide to complete my course of study at CFNI.

The president of CFNI was a godly woman named Freda Lindsey. As the graduates at the commissioning service walked across the platform, Mrs. Lindsey prayed or spoke a word of prophecy over each one. Dindy remembers very clearly the prophetic words that Mrs. Lindsey spoke over me that day, "I see you ruling; rule with love and with power." In the years since I'm not sure exactly how I have ruled, perhaps in my various roles as professor, editor, and director of the Asia Minor Research Center. But hopefully love and power have characterized my actions and behavior in every place where I've served.

Sam Storms writes:

"On the last night of the conference in Houston, Paul Cain called me out of the audience and delivered a ten-minute prophetic word of encouragement. The text he used was from Isaiah 58. In the course of his message, during which he had been speaking of my ministry and how God wanted to use me, he paused. He said, 'Sam, I know you have thought, 'Who's going to take care of me? If I give my life to pastoral ministry, if I deny myself and take up my cross, who will watch over me?' Sam, the Lord says to you, 'I will guide *you* personally. I *will* guide you personally; I will take care of you. I will guide thee continually.' This very pointed application of the first phrase in Isaiah 58:11 was then followed by Paul quoting the rest of the verse, '. . . and satisfy your desire in scorched places, and make your bones strong; and you shall be like a watered garden, like a spring of water, whose waters do not fail.'

At the time, I didn't fully appreciate Paul's words and thought it was nice. But I couldn't make much sense of its application. After all, this was March of 1993. I was committed to the ministry in Ardmore. I had no intention of leaving. Our family was happy and the church was prospering.

Joining a Vineyard church was the farthest thing from my mind. Immediately after the meeting, Jack Deere came to me and said, 'Sam, you may not understand fully what Paul said, but get a videotape of it and write it down. It will probably take on new meaning in a few months.' As it turned out, Jack's advice was right on target, almost to the very day!

Let me jump forward to August of 1993, for now I want to tell you what happened on the day we moved. Moving day was August 18, 1993. It was one of the most demanding and depressing days of my life. Making the decision to leave our church family in Ardmore was among the most difficult I had ever made. When the time finally arrived for us to say goodbye, it was almost more than I could bear. We had spent the day before helping the movers load our belongings and saying our farewells to family and friends. We were scheduled to meet the movers at our new residence in Kansas City at three in the afternoon. It was very early Wednesday morning, August 18th. I was depressed and worried that I had made a terrible mistake. I was fearful of the new responsibilities, both financial and occupational, that I was to assume upon our arrival in Kansas City. Ann was tired and apprehensive. Our daughters were just tired.

Melanie was in the car with me. Ann and Joanna were in the minivan. As Melanie rubbed the sleep from her eyes, she opened a going-away gift she had received from the principal of her school. It was one of those verse-a-day calendars that people set on their kitchen counters or on their bedstand. Needing more than a little encouragement, but with no expectation I'd receive any, I said, 'Well, Melanie, this is as big a day as we've ever had. We're moving to Kansas City. What's our verse for today?' She opened the calendar and turned to August 18th.

If you haven't figured it out yet, the verse for that day was . . . Isaiah 58:11! This was the precise verse the Lord had given Paul Cain as a special promise to me at the conference in Houston, virtually five months to the day (as Jack Deere had 'unwittingly prophesied'). I felt like I had been hit with a bolt of lightning. Slamming on the brakes, I jumped out of the car and ran back on the shoulder of the highway to Ann who was probably thinking that I had changed my mind about the move. I shouted, 'Ann, you'll never guess what has happened. Today is the day. We're moving. We're stepping out in faith. And look at what verse is for today!'

I have no idea how many thousands of verses there are in the Bible. But I do know there are 365 days in the year. You tell me: What are the odds of that *one* verse appearing on that *one* day? They are astronomical, no doubt. But to a God who controls the universe and speaks through his people whom he has gifted prophetically, it is a mere trifle. To me, it was stunning, supernatural confirmation that indeed we had heard the Lord correctly and were doing his will."[2]

Reflection Questions

How was personal prophecy handled by the believers trying to provide guidance to Paul?

What was the human response of the bystanders when they heard these prophecies?

Why is Agabus a model of how personal prophecy should function?

What was Paul's response to these personal prophecies?

Have you ever received a personal prophecy that provided useful guidance to you?

---

2. Storms, *Convergence*, 54, and used with permission.

6

The Journey to Jerusalem and Caesarea

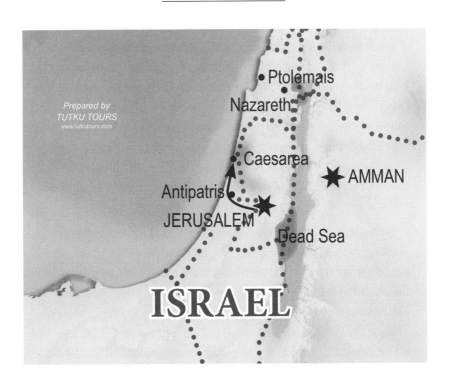

LESSON 17

God uses our religious, civic, and national identities to guide us.

[17] When we arrived at Jerusalem, the brothers and sisters received us warmly. . . . [37] As the soldiers were about to take Paul into the barracks, he asked the commander, "May I say something to you?" "Do you speak Greek?" he replied . . . . [39] Paul answered, "I am a Jew, from Tarsus in Cilicia, a citizen of no ordinary city. Please let me speak to the people . . .." [2] When they heard him speak to them in Aramaic, they became very quiet. Then Paul said: [3] "I am a Jew, born in Tarsus of Cilicia, but brought up in this city. I studied under Gamaliel and was thoroughly trained in the law of our ancestors." (21:17, 37, 39; 22:2–3)

[25] As they stretched him out to flog him, Paul said to the centurion standing there, "Is it legal for you to flog a Roman citizen who hasn't even been found guilty?" [26] When the centurion heard this, he went to the commander and reported it. "What are you going to do?" he asked. "This man is a Roman citizen." [27] The commander went to Paul and asked, "Tell me, are you a Roman citizen?" "Yes, I am," he answered. [28] Then the commander said, "I had to pay a big price for my citizenship." "But I was born a citizen," Paul replied. [29] Those who were about to question him withdrew immediately. The commander himself was alarmed when he realized that he had put Paul, a Roman citizen, in chains. (22:25–29)

[6] Then Paul, knowing that some of them were Sadducees and the others Pharisees, called out in the Sanhedrin, "My brothers, I am a Pharisee, the

son of a Pharisee. I stand on trial because of my hope in the resurrection of the dead." [7] When he said this, a dispute broke out between the Pharisees and the Sadducees, and the assembly was divided. (23:6–7)

[8] Then Paul made his defense: "I have done nothing wrong against the Jewish law or against the temple or against Caesar." [9] Festus, wishing to do the Jews a favor, said to Paul, "Are you willing to go up to Jerusalem and stand trial before me there on these charges?" [10] Paul answered: "I am now standing before Caesar's court, where I ought to be tried. I have not done any wrong to the Jews, as you yourself know very well. [11] If, however, I am guilty of doing anything deserving death, I do not refuse to die. But if the charges brought against me by these Jews are not true, no one has the right to hand me over to them. I appeal to Caesar!" [12] After Festus had conferred with his council, he declared: "You have appealed to Caesar. To Caesar you will go!" (25:8–12)

Paul's Guidance

Luke's narrative, which has been clipping along through the first twenty chapters, suddenly slows down in chapters 21–26. (I would encourage you to read these chapters now since what follows summarizes key moments in them.) These chapters contain a number of speeches by Paul as well as by Jewish and Roman officials that deal with judicial issues related to his arrest in Jerusalem and imprisonment in Caesarea. These scenes of lawyers and hearings drag out for over two years (24:27).

Paul's arrival in Jerusalem became well known both inside and outside the church. Warned by fellow believers not to go there, Paul was nevertheless compelled by the Spirit to deliver the collection for the saints, a benevolent act not mentioned in Acts. Shortly after, Paul was persuaded to go to the temple to join in the purification rites and pay the expenses of four Jewish believers who had made vows (21:23–24). However, Jewish troublemakers from the province of Asia charged that Paul had taken Trophimus, his Gentile traveling companion from Ephesus (21:29), past the barrier that separated Jews from Gentiles. This false accusation that Paul had violated the temple's sacred space nevertheless stirred up the crowd against him.

The Romans maintained a garrison in the Antonia Fortress that overlooked the temple to watch the crowds and control any disturbance that might break out. Soon a riot involving Paul developed, and a cohort of soldiers entered the temple area and took Paul into custody. Seeking to clarify his identity, Paul told the commander in Greek that he was a citizen of the illustrious city of Tarsus in Cilicia. Citizenship in a Greek city was a high honor that Jews occasionally received, and Paul's family had probably been citizens since 171 BC when Tarsus was re-founded by the Seleucid king Antiochus IV. Citizenship had certain wealth requirements, which undoubtedly suggested to the commander that Paul came from an elite family. So when Paul asked him for permission to address the crowd, the commander granted his request.

When Paul began to speak Aramaic, this switch in languages caught the crowd's attention, for they suspected that he was a Diaspora Jew who could only speak Greek. How did Paul learn Aramaic, the everyday language of Judea and its cognate, Hebrew, the religious language of Judaism? Paul suggests that it was in his home at Tarsus that he learned these languages, being raised a "Hebrew of Hebrews" (Phil 3:5). He would have perfected his language skills while living in Jerusalem where he was taught by one of the leading rabbis of his day, Gamaliel. It seems that Paul was not averse to name dropping. Mentioning Gamaliel was like declaring he was educated at Harvard under a Nobel laureate. His audience was suitably impressed until Paul stated that on the road to Damascus Jesus had commissioned him to go to the Gentiles. Literally all hell broke loose then, and the Roman soldiers were barely able to rescue him.

The Romans were now curious regarding the identity of this troublemaker and determined to learn the cause of this uproar by flogging Paul. But as the soldier lifted his whip, Paul pulled out his get-out-of-jail-free card—Roman citizenship. At Philippi he never announced this fact initially (16:22–24; 37–38), but on this occasion Paul immediately declared that he was a Roman citizen. After the commander was summoned, the conversation became a bit humorous. The commander told how he had bought his citizenship, but Paul trumped him by declaring he was born a citizen.[1] This brought an immediate reaction: the soldiers jumped back in fear. They had wrongfully seized a Roman citizen, which could have serious legal consequences. Once Paul had established his identity, he knew he was in safe hands at least temporarily.

1. For further discussion about Paul's Greek and Roman citizenship see my article, "Was Paul a Cilician?"

The next day he was brought before the Sanhedrin, where the charges against him were presented by the high priest Ananias. Quickly perceiving the factions lined up against him, he utilized a divide-and-conquer strategy to work in his favor. Informing the gathering that his family had been Pharisees for generations, he claimed that the charges were based on his belief in the resurrection of the dead, a doctrine in which the Sadducees didn't believe. This, of course, gained him the support of the other Pharisees who turned their hostility from Paul to the Sadducees. The Roman commander, realizing that Paul was again in danger from this religious fracas, snatched him from their midst and incarcerated him once again in the fortress (23:8–10).

The following night the Lord appeared to Paul to reassure him: "Take courage! As you have testified about me in Jerusalem, so you must also testify in Rome." Whether this guidance was in a dream or vision is not stated. This must have been encouraging because soon his nephew brought news of a plot against Paul's life. When the commander was told, he sent Paul to the provincial capital Caesarea under the protection of seventy horsemen and two hundred spearmen. Being a Roman citizen certainly had its benefits pertaining to safety and security (23:11–24).

Paul remained under a loose house arrest in the palace of the governor Felix. He refused to return to Jerusalem for a trial, knowing that it meant certain death. After two years a new governor Festus arrived in Judea. Seeking to gain favor with the Jewish leaders, he promised to hold a tribunal in Caesarea to review the charges against this troublesome prisoner. Appearing before Festus and the Jews, Paul argued that the proper venue for his case was here and not in Jerusalem. When pressed to return to Jerusalem, he appealed to Caesar, his right as a Roman citizen. The drama was over for now; Festus' hands were tied because the prisoner had appealed to Caesar. Later when Paul appeared before Festus, King Agrippa II, and his sister Berenice, they determined that Paul neither deserved imprisonment nor death. In fact, Paul could have been set free. But since he had appealed to Caesar, Roman law required that the prisoner be sent to Rome for his day in court (23:26–23:32).

These chapters present Paul as a defendant forced to exercise sagacity and diligence to survive the charges against him. And he does so by using his multiple identities: in Judaism as a Pharisee who studied under Gamaliel; in the Greek city as a citizen of Tarsus; and in the Roman Empire as a citizen of Rome. Before his various audiences he is able to switch languages from Aramaic to Greek and probably even to Latin. As we have seen, Paul does not flaunt these identities indiscriminately but draws on them in crucial situations to ensure his survival. There was perhaps no other person alive in the first century with such a blend of identities, a key reason why Jesus called Paul to be his unique apostle.

Guidance Today

Dindy and I are keenly aware of what a privilege it is to be Americans and to hold a U.S. passport. When we travel internationally, an entry visa is often unnecessary. As we apply periodically for our residence permits in Turkey, our American citizenship is a positive factor in facilitating their approval. Through the foresight and decisions of our ancestors, we happened to be born in the United States; it was not our choice.

My great grandparents Olof and Christina emigrated from Sweden to Minnesota in 1891. They met in July of that year, and one night two months later eloped to America. Christina was only eighteen years old while Olof was forty-one. My grandfather Tony (Anton) was born in 1893, the second of eleven children and the first to survive infancy. In Dindy's case her father Albert with his parents and siblings moved from Paris to New York City in the early 1900s arriving through Ellis Island. The family of her mother Florence also came to New York because of pogroms against the Jews in Russia in the 1880s. Dindy's parents also had a significant age difference: Albert was twenty-two years older than Florence. When Dindy was born, he was fifty-eight years old and she was thirty-six.

Dindy's father was a doctor who commuted each day from Manhattan to his office in New Jersey. Her mother was a music teacher in the prestigious High School of Music and Art in Manhattan, which Dindy and her sister Phoebe both attended. A station agent for the Soo Line Railroad, my father Wayne only had a high school education. My mother Marilyn was a librarian who taught in an elementary school for several years after receiving her teaching degree. My two sisters, Marla and Mari Beth, were three and nine years younger respectively. So in family birth order, Dindy and I are both first-born children.

Higher education was easily accessible to us. Dindy received her B.A. at Queens College, part of the City University of New York. As a city resident her education was free. My B.A. was from Trinity Bible College, one of the many private Christian colleges located in America. We both received our M.A. degrees at Regent University. When we attended Regent in the 1980s, the university was giving 75% tuition waivers for qualified students. This was a godsend for us, since we were both working full time as well as raising a family. So we were able to graduate without any debt. My doctoral program at the University of South Africa was very affordable, since its fees were geared towards African students. Tuition for four years of enrollment was around $10,000, the normal cost of one year of tuition in an American program. I was the first person in my family ever to earn a doctoral degree. Our education, like Paul's, has been used by the Holy Spirit to guide us to various positions and places unobtainable without the requisite academic qualifications (see Lesson 5).

Regarding language, we are largely monolingual like most Americans. Although Dindy's father grew up speaking French, German, and Yiddish, he did not speak them at home. She studied French in high school and college, and after her junior year traveled in France. I have also studied French and German but more as reading languages. Of course, we have picked up some Turkish while living in Turkey. So we are fortunate that English has become the lingua franca in the world today. We can travel almost anywhere and find someone with whom we can speak.

What an incredible open door that English speakers have today! Everyone wants to learn our language, especially American English. Dindy continues to serve as a conversation facilitator for English learners at the St. Paul Cultural Center. She has helped prospective pilots, doctoral students, and others who want to improve their English conversational skills or need to pass language tests required for employment. Soon after our arrival in Antalya I was asked by a local research center to serve as the English editor for its publications. So God has used our English proficiency to open up opportunities to use these skills. Our unique religious, civic, and national backgrounds have played an important role in how God has guided us.

Dindy Wilson writes:

"Raised in a Jewish home in Manhattan, New York City, I had almost no familiarity with the New Testament or with Jesus' life and teachings. It was a slow process for me to accept that Jesus is God after being convinced for so long that such a belief was taboo. Even later after accepting Jesus' divinity, it took time for me to adjust to this 'non-Jewish' way of thinking and believing. This is not to say that I didn't feel close to God as a child.

My mother had virtually rejected her upbringing and famously said, 'I always pray before exams!' But my father continued with his faith privately and kept his prayer book and shawl in his top dresser drawer away from our prying eyes. At some point in my growing up years I told my father that I was afraid of the dark and needed some help. He pulled out his prayer book and taught me a prayer to say each night. I must have been a loyal follower because I 'religiously' repeated it nightly for years! Not only did it give me a sense of security but it also awakened me to God's presence in my life.

One day soon after that lesson from my father and the ensuing awareness of a heavenly Father, I remember walking on a street near our apartment on the Upper West Side. I don't recall having any particular problem, but I remember looking up at the sky and having a strong feeling that God was there and that he was watching over me. Years later, when I became a believer at age 30, I remember saying to Jesus, 'so that was *You* whom I "saw" when I was a child!' It was truly a 'My Lord and my God' experience!' (John 20:28). So I was not unfamiliar with God the Father, but as I said earlier, I had no knowledge of Christ.

One of the steps to my encountering Jesus involved some Bible studies with Pastor Ted Standing Elk and his wife Mamie on South Dakota's Pine Ridge Indian Reservation. They were faithful prayer warriors who knelt in the living room of their government housing and prayed for all of us in the Native American Church. They invited us to their Bible studies, and since we all considered ourselves Christians, we agreed to attend. I remember Pastor Ted saying that God had once 'spoken' a Bible verse to him that he had not known before. So perhaps that prepared me for my own memorable experience soon after!

It happened as I awoke early one morning in 1974 in our log cabin in Porcupine on the reservation. As a brand new believer whose mind was virtually a 'clean slate' regarding Christian things, I was startled by a 'voice' that I heard as I slowly came awake: 'Be ye near me even as I am near you!' I really had no idea who was speaking or what that meant. Imagine my surprise when later I discovered that James 4:8 says, 'Come near to God and he will come near to you.' From that day to this I marvel at my encounter with God and still seek to follow that heavenly call!"

God uses our religious, civic, and national identities to guide us.

Jonathan Shirey writes:

"A few year ago, my wife and I sensed that God was asking us to invest into the lives of younger people seeking to grow in the Lord Jesus. We wanted to do this through an intense five-month program that involved teaching, mentoring, cultural exposure, and practical ministry experience. Discipleship Beyond was born, and we began to seek young followers of Jesus interested in serving him in every circumstance of life. We desired to foster an active compassion for the lost while living in obedience and sacrifice within a biblical worldview.

The program kicks off with an intensive twelve-week session called Formation. Among the topics addressed are the Lordship of Jesus and Hearing God's Voice. Following Formation, participants are sent on a ten- to twelve-week outreach in another country. This practicum condenses all they have learned into hands-on service toward others. Because our participants are drawn from many nations, we have faced several challenges in selecting destinations for our outreach time. Some countries have differing visa requirements for entry based upon one's nationality.

Recently we faced an unusual situation. Just four weeks away from our departure for outreach, we were forced to cancel the planned destination because our hosts cancelled for health reasons. We were left scrambling for a solution and faced a major hurdle because of the multinational make-up of our group. We still had seven to eight opportunities available; however, in order to keep our group together, we were forced to cross a number of them off of the list. There was simply no way to obtain visas for all participants in the amount of time available. When the dust settled, our group found themselves serving in Eastern Europe. Each member affirmed their joy and assurance that circumstance had guided us into God's will for our team."

Reflection Questions

What religious, civic, and national identities does Paul mention in Acts?

Why do you think Paul claimed his Roman citizenship in Jerusalem?

What was Paul's defense strategy before the Sanhedrin?

How did the Holy Spirit use Paul's national identity to get him to Rome?

What are your unique identities that God could use to guide you in future endeavors?

7

The Journey to Rome

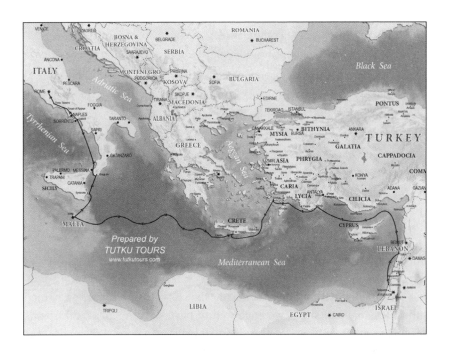

LESSON 18

God uses faulty decision making to guide us.

⁹ Much time had been lost, and sailing had already become dangerous because by now it was after the Day of Atonement. So Paul warned them, ¹⁰ "Men, I can see that our voyage is going to be disastrous and bring great loss to ship and cargo, and to our own lives also." ¹¹ But the centurion, instead of listening to what Paul said, followed the advice of the pilot and of the owner of the ship. ¹² Since the harbor was unsuitable to winter in, the majority decided that we should sail on, hoping to reach Phoenix and winter there. This was a harbor in Crete, facing both southwest and northwest. (27:9–12)

Paul's Guidance

For the first time in Acts, Paul was not making an extended journey as a free man. Because of his appeal to Caesar, Paul was placed on a coasting vessel along with other prisoners in the custody of a centurion named Julius. Prisoners of status were allowed to have slaves or personal friends serving as attendants, and a Thessalonian believer named Aristarchus was accompanying him in that capacity. Aristarchus had ministered with Paul in Ephesus (19:29) and was among the men who accompanied Paul to Jerusalem with the collection from the Gentile churches (20:4). Aristarchus had apparently stayed in Judea and might also have served Paul during his two-year imprisonment in Caesarea.

This is the final "we" section, so what follows is a firsthand description of the dramatic events. Because of prevailing headwinds, the coasting vessel was forced to follow the coastline of southern Asia Minor passing the regions of Cilicia and Pamphylia until reaching Andriake, the unmentioned port of Myra in Lycia. (Several centuries later Myra was to become famous as the city where St. Nicholas served as bishop.) Because their vessel planned to sail north along the Aegean coast to Adramyttium, Julius needed to secure passage for his prisoners and their attendants on a vessel bound for Rome.

A large grain ship that had come from Alexandria was in port with space available for Julius's group. Why was this ship laden with grain now in Myra, and why was it traveling at this time of year? Because of prevailing winds, especially in late autumn, ships coming from North Africa could not sail directly northwest to Italy across the Mediterranean. Like the smaller coasting vessel, this super tanker was forced to hug the Mediterranean coastline of Palestine and Asia Minor as far as possible.

Grain ships typically did not sail so late in the season. But ship owners, captains, and crews sometimes took the risk of bringing a second cargo of grain to Rome later in the year. If successful, they could make large profits because of the inflated prices related to the hazards of winter delivery. This grain ship had likely made one round-trip already from Italy to Alexandria and was now attempting a second passage. As Paul boarded the ship, he probably thought the captain intended to find a safe port to ride out the winter since it was so late in the season. Little did he know that events would prove otherwise.

Although the distance was not great from Myra to Cnidus, a port at the southwestern tip of Asia Minor, strong headwinds delayed the ship's progress. Unable to continue across the open sea toward Greece, the ship turned southwest towards the island of Crete. Arriving on its leeward (southern) side, the ship found shelter in the protected harbor at Fair Havens. The slow progress thus far had placed their arrival after the Day of Atonement, which in AD 59 fell on October 5. Because of his previous nautical experience and knowledge of the dangers of sailing late in the year, Paul warned his shipmates that their Mediterranean voyage would end in disaster if they continued. Since Fair Havens was unsuitable as a winter anchorage, the captain and ship owner, with the consent of the centurion, opted to take the risk and sail on. Undoubtedly the centurion was offered a share of the profits to induce a favorable decision. However, Paul's warning proved prophetic.

The first-person description of the storm and wreck is one of the most gripping either in ancient or modern literature. Its accurate description of the ship, its equipment, and the crew's behavior tell us much about navigation in antiquity. The ship owner, the captain, and the centurion had made the faulty decision to proceed, despite knowing the risk. Paul and his companions, through no choice of their own, were forced to accept it. Luke describes the hurricane-force wind as *typhōnikos* (27:14), whose English derivative is typhoon. Living directly on the Mediterranean Sea in Antalya, Dindy and I have experienced winter storms with similar typhoon-like winds. As our building was shaking violently, we have given thanks that we were not aboard a ship like Paul.

Verses 13–20 describe the attempts to save the ship during the many days that the storm raged. Undoubtedly seasick, the passengers and crew had little appetite for food. From a natural perspective the bad decision to sail prompted this prognosis: "We finally gave up all hope of being saved" (27:20). However, the Lord had appeared to Paul over two years earlier and given him this promise: "As you have testified about me in Jerusalem, so you must also testify in Rome" (23:11). During these precarious days Paul must have reminded himself and his companions of the Lord's assurance. Despite the faulty decisions aboard ship that now threatened their lives, they clung to the hope that God would somehow bring them safely to Rome.

Guidance Today

I had never been fired from a job before, but because of a poor decision on my part, there was to be a first time. But first some back story. During my time of study in Dallas, I started to work part-time at a nearby Montgomery Ward store as a tire salesman in the automotive department. The Lord blessed my sales efforts there, and along with some part-time work I was able to provide for our family. When we moved to Virginia Beach to begin graduate studies at Regent University, Dindy and I both needed to work full time to support our growing family. But I was determined not to sell tires at Wards again. I was over it and decided that God had a better job for me.

Since I had driven Volvo automobiles for years and was a good salesman, I applied at a nearby Volvo dealer for a sales position. Although the management told me that my work schedule could be fitted around my class schedule, I soon learned this was not possible. The hours of my Greek class began to conflict with work. Thinking the need for income to be more important, I decided to put off the class for another year. But the Volvo dealership was making its own decision: they didn't want a full-time student as an employee. Soon after arriving at work one day, I was told that I had been fired. At the time I thought it was their bad decision, but later came to realize that the faulty decision was my own. For my degree plan the Greek class was imperative, so from an academic perspective my firing worked out for the good.

However, I was still determined not to work at Montgomery Ward so I took a job as a counselor at a group home for delinquent young men. By working the graveyard shift, I reasoned that I could study while the boys were all asleep. After taking the job I quickly discovered that early bedtimes were not the rule so I wasn't getting much studying done. Plus I was struggling to get my body clock adjusted to working all night. One evening a young resident approached the desk where I was reading and hit me on the head with a wooden 2x4 from a door frame. I never saw it coming. Other boys reported the incident, and I was taken unconscious to a local hospital where the gash was stitched up. After staying overnight for observation, I was released the next day and sent home with a sore head to recover. Needless to say, I decided not to return to that job.

I had run out of job options, so you can probably guess what happened next. I contacted the Montgomery Ward at Lynnhaven Mall in Virginia Beach and learned that there was a job opening for a tire salesman. Soon I was selling tires again with God blessing me financially in commissioned sales. The job was perfect: I could schedule my hours around my classes and family activities without a problem. For five years (it seemed forever sometimes), I worked at Wards while both Dindy and I finished our Master's degrees at Regent University. When the job of theological writer for the Living By The Book project opened up at CBN in 1989, I was extremely delighted to move on from automotive sales. But I was also aware how my faulty decisions had initially delayed God's will being realized in my life and family.

M. Blaine Smith writes:

"When I was twenty-five, I took an afternoon to pray and mull over God's direction for my life in a pleasant mountain park setting. Since I was eager for marriage at this time in my life (as I'd been at most previous times), my reflecting naturally wandered into this arena as I pondered the future. For whatever reasons, my thoughts began to focus on a young woman in the college fellowship of my church whom I barely knew. I mused over what it might be like to be married to her. I was surprised to realize how attracted I was to this possibility. As the mental image of her as my wife came into sharper focus, I was certain that God was giving me a vision of the years to come. I knew I'd been ordained to marital bliss with this young lady.

For some time after that I cherished the belief that I'd been privy to a private screening on God's future plan for my life. The dream of being married to her naturally blossomed and grew. It finally came to a screeching halt one evening when I had the audacity to share my "vision" with her, and she bluntly told me that God hadn't spoken to her in any such way.

Well, not exactly a screeching halt, because for some months after that I did continue to hope that she would eventually come to her senses and see God's will as I did. Gradually, though, reality sank in (especially when she became engaged to someone else), and I began to accept that I might have taken more guidance from those mental ruminations on the mountain than was justified.

I now believe that God did indeed guide me during that time on the mountain. The guidance, though, wasn't for the future but *for the present*. He was allowing me to get a better handle on some feelings that I hadn't previously understood.

He was letting me see that I was attracted to this woman, or at least intrigued with her. These feelings *might* indicate that I should take some steps to develop a friendship with her or even ask her for a date. Or they might simply be feelings and nothing more. In any case, they were in no remote way a promise from God about the years ahead. They were not a pledge from God that she would even accept a date, let alone agree to betrothal. They were merely light unto my path—the path of better understanding my emotional sides."[1]

Reflection Questions

Why was it dangerous to sail on the Mediterranean Sea during the fall and winter?

For what reason did the pilot and ship owner want to continue the voyage?

---

1. Smith, *Knowing God's Will*, 37–38, and used with permission.

God uses faulty decision making to guide us.

What was Paul's advice to them as well as to the centurion guarding him?

Why did Paul have confidence that he and his companions would reach Rome?

Can you remember when a faulty decision affected you or others close to you?

LESSON 19

God uses angels to guide us.

[21] After they had gone a long time without food, Paul stood up before them and said: "Men, you should have taken my advice not to sail from Crete; then you would have spared yourselves this damage and loss. [22] But now I urge you to keep up your courage, because not one of you will be lost; only the ship will be destroyed. [23] Last night an angel of the God to whom I belong and whom I serve stood beside me [24] and said, 'Do not be afraid, Paul. You must stand trial before Caesar; and God has graciously given you the lives of all who sail with you.' [25] So keep up your courage, men, for I have faith in God that it will happen just as he told me. [26] Nevertheless, we must run aground on some island." (27:21–26)

Paul's Guidance

Because of the faulty decision to set sail late in the season, Paul and his 275 companions on the ship had given up hope of rescue. But the Lord had given Paul a promise that he would reach Rome, and the remainder of chapter 27 chronicles how God saved the day. One stormy morning Paul stood up in the midst of the fatigued and starved crew and gave them an "I told you so" exhortation. How well his words were received cannot be known. But knowing human nature, there was probably a ripple of disgruntlement like: "Be quiet, Paul, tell us something we don't already know." His next sentence, however, must have both shocked and comforted them. No one would lose their life; only the ship would be lost. He then described the angelic visitation during the previous night. The angel, after telling Paul not to be afraid, reminded him of the promise that he must appear before Caesar in Rome. As part of this promise, God would spare the lives of all his companions.

The ancients, especially sailors, were very superstitious and often prayed to various deities for protection on their sea journeys and for a safe return home. Archaeological evidence showing that even Jews and Christians did this comes from the Greek island of Syros. Carved into rocks near the harbor by both groups are prayers for help at the beginning of a voyage or of thanksgiving at its successful conclusion. Sixteen Christian inscriptions invoke the words, "Lord, help. . .." Two Jewish prayers, known from the menorahs inscribed next to them, read: "Lord, help your servant and the ship's crew of Naxians" and "In the name of the living god, Heortylis returned safely from a good voyage." Paul's pagan companions would thus have no qualms about accepting such a supernatural sign and announcement that Paul's God had promised to save them. Nevertheless, Paul encouraged the men to remain strong because the ordeal wasn't over. For the damaged ship still needed to run aground on some island for them to be saved. It is worth noting again that something natural (running aground) had to occur for the supernatural (angelic promise) to be fulfilled.

The drama continues through the rest of the chapter with its nail-biting action. As the ship approached land in the darkness, the crew, despite Paul's promise of safety, decided to take the desperate situation into their own hands. They were going to jump ship and abandon everyone else to their own fate. Paul recognized what was happening and informed Julius and the other soldiers. He realized that their rescue required the manpower and expertise of the sailors. This time the centurion listened to Paul, and the lifeboat's rope was cut to prevent the crew's escape (27:27–32).

In the dawn twilight on the fourteenth day of the storm, Paul urged everyone to eat some food to gain strength for the final approach to land. No doubt many had lost their appetite due to seasickness, and the preparation of hot meals was difficult because of the rough seas. Once again Paul reminded everyone that if they stuck together, no lives would be lost. In an act typical of a Jewish or Christian prayer of thanksgiving and reminiscent of the Lord's Supper, Paul stood before the gathered assembly, broke bread, and thanked God for their deliverance. Everyone aboard was strengthened and encouraged. How wheat was ground and bread baked was a miracle in itself, but bread was supplied and everyone ate (27:33–38).

Remarkably the ordeal was still not over. Everyone began to throw sacks of grain overboard to lighten the load. This was the precious cargo that was going to bring riches to the ship owner, captain, and sailors. It must have been a bittersweet moment as they tossed these sacks into the sea. Through a series of maneuvers including cutting the anchors, the sailors caused the ship to drift into the bay of an island now in view. Running aground, the ship began to break apart in the surf.

Suddenly the soldiers panicked and decided to kill all the prisoners including Paul. Like the guard in the Philippian jail (16:27), the soldiers realized that they would be held liable if their prisoners escaped. Like the sailors, they had forgotten Paul's promise that all would be saved if they cooperated. Fortunately Paul had favor with Julius, who had come to believe Paul's declarations. He prevented the soldiers from killing the prisoners and instead ordered everyone to abandon ship. Some swam to land, while others clutched planks and other debris to drift to shore (27:39–44). The chapter closes with the confirmation of the angel's word: "Everyone reached land safely" (27:44).

Guidance Today

I have never met an angel or had one speak to me. Nevertheless, I have sensed the presence of angels at various times in my life, usually while driving. While I was teaching at the Central Indian Bible College from 1982–1984, I often spoke in behalf of the school at Assembly of God churches in the Dakotas and Montana. Sometimes on the late-night drives through the Badlands and across the prairies, I would grow sleepy and begin to nod off. I can remember several times when it seemed like an angelic presence intervened to awaken me or to steer the car back on to the road to keep me out of the ditch. On other occasions when an accident seemed imminent, I have cried out to the Lord, and an angel seemed to intervene by miraculously moving my vehicle out of harm's way.

One morning while traveling in Turkey, I departed from the capital Ankara to visit Pessinus. I had never visited this Galatian city before so could only estimate how to get there from a map. The intercity bus dropped me off along the highway at Sivrihisar, the closest town. From the local bus garage I could usually catch a minibus to area villages, in this case to Ballıhisar. A young woman conservatively dressed in a headscarf also got off the bus. Looking around, I saw a taxi stand in the distance so walked over there to seek assistance. In those days I spoke little Turkish. Arriving there and obviously a bit perplexed, I pondered what to do next. Out of the blue the young woman approached me and asked in perfect English if she could help me. I told her of my need to find a minibus to Ballıhisar. After discussing this with the taxi driver, she told me no buses ran there and that I needed to go to Pessinus by taxi. She negotiated a price with the driver who would wait while I visited the ancient site and then bring me back to catch a bus to Eskişehir. I thanked her profusely and put my bag in the taxi to depart. As I watched her walk away, I was astounded at the Lord's timing. Whether she was an angel or not, she certainly appeared to me at the precise moment I needed help.[1]

Sam Storms writes:

"Our first few months in Kansas City were incredibly difficult. Ann's dream which indicated that I would have a particularly hard time of it was all too painfully true. I knew we were supposed to be at Metro Vineyard Fellowship. I never doubted the clarity of God's call. So I'm not suggesting that what I'm about to describe is normative for every believer. All I know is what God graciously did for Ann and me in a time of desperation.

One night in early November, 1993, I had gone to bed about 11:00. I'm an especially sound sleeper. Virtually nothing can wake me up. Ann had unintentionally fallen asleep in Joanna's room after having put her to bed. At about 1:00 a.m. Ann woke up and walked back into our bedroom. There above the headboard, as she describes it, was the outline of what looked like an angel. Since Ann had never seen an angel before, she quickly dismissed the possibility and got in bed.

You must understand, of course, that I only know this because she later told me. I was sound asleep. But I was dreaming. In my dream I heard the unmistakable and distinctive sound of four chimes. The melody was

---

1. Guidance by angels requires additional caution because of possible abuse due to overemphasizing their role with believers. Sometimes in popular teaching angels are elevated almost over Jesus and the Holy Spirit. For my mentor's helpful overview, see Williams, "Angels on Assignment."

clear and pristine. The experience was so profound that, uncharacteristically, I woke up. Just as I was coming out of my sleep, I felt Ann's fingernails digging into my arm. 'Did you hear the chimes?' she asked in a quivering voice. 'Yeah. But how could *you* hear what *I* was dreaming?' By this time we were both *wide* awake!

The idea that Ann had heard with her physical ears what I heard only in my mind was enough to bring me completely out of my slumber. I immediately said: 'Did the chimes sound like this . . . ?' at which point I quietly repeated for her the brief melody. Her fingernails dug even deeper into my flesh. 'Yes! What do we do now?'

Being the theologian that I am, I said: 'I don't know. What do you think?' 'I think we ought to pray,' she responded with great profundity. We did. Later Ann told me that the chimes sounded as if they were coming from over by the door to our bedroom, some twenty feet away. As for me, they were in my head.

Skeptics will try to dismiss it all as just so much hyper-spirituality. I can't do anything about that. I can only tell you in the integrity of my heart what we experienced. You have to make up your own mind. But Ann and I are convinced beyond doubt that we were the recipients of an angelic visitation. No words were spoken, but the room and our hearts were filled with awe and fear and an increased awareness of God's presence and power.

A few months later, Ann was still wondering why it all happened. So she asked the Lord. His answer was simple and to the point: 'To give you courage.' Of course! If we needed anything at that time, it was the courage to persevere, the courage to press on, the courage to hold fast to what we knew was God's leading in our move to Kansas City.

We don't live each day with the expectation of an angelic visitation. We don't make our decisions based on supernatural experiences like the ones I've described. We look first and fundamentally to the written Word of God. But we do bow before the God of heaven and earth and say, 'Thank you, we love you. We praise you for these tokens of your presence and the encouragement they bring.'"[2]

Reflection Questions

How do you think Paul's words were received aboard the floundering ship?

2. Storms, *Convergence*, 73, and used with permission.

God uses angels to guide us.

Why do you think God sent an angel to Paul at this time?

What message did the angel speak to Paul, and how was it linked to a previous promise?

How did supernatural and natural elements play out in the rescue of Paul and his shipmates?

If you have experienced an angelic presence or been guided by an angel, describe it briefly.

LESSON 20

God uses fellow believers to guide us.

¹¹ After three months we put out to sea in a ship that had wintered in the island. It was an Alexandrian ship with the figurehead of the twin gods Castor and Pollux. ¹² We put in at Syracuse and stayed there three days. ¹³ From there we set sail and arrived at Rhegium. The next day the south wind came up, and on the following day we reached Puteoli. ¹⁴ There we found some brothers and sisters who invited us to spend a week with them. And so we came to Rome. ¹⁵ The brothers and sisters there had heard that we were coming, and they traveled as far as the Forum of Appius and the Three Taverns to meet us. At the sight of these people Paul thanked God and was encouraged. ¹⁶ When we got to Rome, Paul was allowed to live by himself, with a soldier to guard him. (28:11–16)

Paul's Guidance

After surviving the shipwreck and spending three winter months on Malta, Paul must have looked forward to his arrival in Rome. He had written to the Roman church almost three years before announcing his intention to visit. Thinking then that he would arrive as a free man, he was instead coming as a prisoner. A second grain ship, which had wintered in Malta's sheltered Grand Harbor, now became Paul's transport onward. It first docked at Syracuse on the east side of Sicily. The ship then passed through the Strait of Messina before arriving at Rhegium (Reggio Calabria) located at the tip of Italy. Sailing north, it next made port at Puteoli (Pozzoli).

His hospitable reception by the believers there must have greatly encouraged Paul. After visiting for a week, Paul and his party began the three-day journey to Rome on the Via Appia. Apparently a believer in Puteoli had traveled to Rome to announce that Paul had finally arrived in Italy. So when Paul reached the Forum of Appius and the Three Taverns, believers from Rome were present to meet him. Their effort to come and greet him cheered Paul, and he gave thanks for their warm welcome. Paul's guard Julius must have been impressed again with the love and helpfulness displayed by Christians. Together they walked the final leg into Rome entering through the Porta Appia.

In Rome the centurion would first present Paul to the authorities and then hand over the documents from Festus that outlined the charges against the prisoner. Festus undoubtedly noted that the charges brought by the Jewish Sanhedrin were really of a religious nature and were not culpable under Roman law. Since the offenses were not capital in nature, Paul was allowed to rent a private lodging with only one soldier to guard him. Local Christians probably helped him arrange an accommodation that would be accessible to Rome's Christian and Jewish communities. Soon after Paul invited the local Jewish leaders to his home to share the gospel (28:17–29).

Acts closes by stating that Paul continued to live for two years in this rental property. Here he had a continual open house to conduct ministry. The final verse emphatically describes this mission: "He proclaimed the kingdom of God and taught about the Lord Jesus Christ—with all boldness and without hindrance!" (28:31). The Spirit who had first said "Go" at Damascus (9:6; cf. 11, 15) had brought the apostle to the capital and center of the Roman Empire. And Paul's hope and expectation was that the Spirit would again direct him to "Go" from Rome even to Spain.

Guidance Today

Benjamin van Rensburg was the pastor of the Union Church of Istanbul in the 2000s; and whenever we visited this historic city, we attended church there. Over the years I had developed a good rapport with the congregation. Previously Benjamin had invited me to conduct a seminar on the Seven Churches, and we also co-led a UCI tour to eastern Turkey. Our collegial relationship was fostered further because Benjamin was South African, and I had my South African academic connections.

In October 2009 we had just arrived back in the U.S. and were enjoying a week at the beach with our children Winema, Jim, David, and their families. One morning I opened an email, which prompted me to shout to Dindy, "What have you been praying?" The email contained an invitation from Benjamin to serve as the interim pastor at UCI for nine months in 2010–2011. He and his family had decided to take a much-needed sabbatical back in South Africa. Dindy smiled when she heard what Benjamin had written, for she had indeed been praying that a door might open so that we could live in Istanbul for ministry as well as to spend more time with our family there. The reasons we had moved to Izmir were no longer in play. I had never pastored nor desired to do so. But we both immediately sensed that this invitation from Benjamin was God's call. Nevertheless, we still consulted our pastor and friend Bruce Anderson about whether Istanbul or Antalya should be the next step. His wise counsel was: "Maybe you will do one first and then the other." And that's exactly what happened!

For years I had been teaching students preparing for pastoral ministry. Now the Lord seemed to want me to get some pastoral experience for myself. However, I already had some potential complications on my calendar. I was scheduled for two more weeks of excavation at the synagogue in Priene in August 2010, plus I planned to present several papers at the annual biblical studies meetings in Atlanta that November. Benjamin graciously agreed to allow me to honor those commitments, and the agreement was made to come to Istanbul.

In early August 2010 my friend Levent Oral arranged for the Tutku van driven by Yalkın Uca to take us and our belongings to Istanbul. We lived in the pastor's apartment in the Union Han in historic Beyoğlu. Our view was spectacular, looking across the Golden Horn toward the Hagia Sophia and the ships entering the Bosporus. The only downside was the 121 high steps required to reach the apartment, since no elevator was allowed in the historic Union Han. Every half hour was marked with a bell clanging on the historic tram passing down Istiklal Avenue. There was even regular late-night street entertainment, especially from "Howlin' Hannah" who moaned and "played" her guitar into the wee hours. As a native New Yorker Dindy loved Istanbul's big-city life with its constant noise and action. But for a small-town boy like me, it was overwhelming. There was no place to ride my bike or walk in green space, and hordes of people were always jostling on the street.

The big bonus was that each Sunday we saw our grandchildren (and their parents too)! After the church service we hung out together for the rest of the day. Perhaps my biggest highlight as interim pastor was the opportunity to dedicate our granddaughter Bethany who was born in 2010 on my birthday, November 26. An unforeseen benefit of our time in Istanbul was the accessibility of my publisher's office just up the street. So I was easily able to assist in the editorial preparation of my book *Biblical Turkey* that was published in the fall of 2010.

The Van Rensburgs were scheduled to return in late April 2011, so we were faced with the immediate decision as to where to live next. Through the years James and Renata Bultema had been urging us to consider making Antalya our home. They had invited us to preach and teach at St. Paul Union Church as well as to speak at a team retreat. In the same way that God used Benjamin to provide guidance for our move to Istanbul, we felt God was using James and Renata to give direction for our next stage in Turkey. After preaching on Easter April 24, 2011, we said goodbye to the UCI congregation, our family, and Istanbul. The following day we boarded a plane to Antalya. In retrospect, it is interesting to see how our two recent moves resulted from suggestions by fellow believers. Where we go next and how we will be guided there is unknown, but for now we are very content living in Antalya.

Dennis Massaro writes:

"When out of nowhere I was approached to consider spending three months in Turkey to serve as an interim pastor, I was rather shocked and intrigued at the same time. I prayed about it and talked with several people that I knew believed in me and had an intimate relationship with God. I had ap-proached them previously at different junctures in my life for prayer, ad-vice, and wise counsel. And they had always offered me, not exactly what to do, but principles needed to make the right decisions. This time was no different from the rest.

Two months passed, and at the end of a time of meeting with many respected and godly men and women, I decided to take a leave from my job as a mortgage broker and head to Antalya. God used one person to challenge me to consider this opportunity and many others to encourage me to take a risk, trust God, and seek to serve him in a new setting.

The experience was amazing! I loved serving in an international church in Turkey. I was able to use the gifts and abilities that God had given me. I had support from a wide variety of people, and after a break of fourteen years from vocational ministry, I sensed the favor of God as I spent my days investing in the lives of people, preaching, and teaching. After my three months of service was completed, I returned to America to resume life as I had known it in the mortgage business. But God was not finished with me.

A few months after arriving back home, I was approached again and asked if I would consider returning to Turkey on a more permanent basis. Once again I met with the same people I had met with the first time, asking for their input. Because of their involvement in my life, I returned to Antalya for two months the following year with similar responsibilities. With only two weeks remaining in my service that year, I was asked by a well-respected member of the congregation to sit down for a conversation. He challenged me to 'go back to America and do business with God' as he and others were sensing that God might be calling me to move to Turkey to become the senior pastor of this international congregation. Through tears I listened to the challenge and returned to America resolute to meet once again with my trusted advisors and friends for their input. The rest is history!

God used so many people in my life during the entire process. They poured into me; they loved me; they prayed for me; they encouraged and supported me. Their wise counsel and sensitive hearts enabled me to search the Scriptures and listen to the voice of God. With their involvement in my life confirming God's call, I stepped out in faith believing that God had a good plan, and I simply needed to trust him. I sold my home in six days and raised my full financial support in sixty days. I said my goodbyes, packed up, and moved to Antalya, sensing God's favor all along the way.

My journey began as one person approached me with an idea that seemed so out of reach. It continued as person after person poured into my life with their challenges, their wisdom, and their godly advice. I have now served as the full-time pastor for almost three years, and daily I thank God for the way he used scores of men and women in my life to enable me to discern the will of God. His guidance for me has come through the committed lives of some amazing people, and I could not be more thankful."

God uses fellow believers to guide us.

Reflection Questions

How did the believers in Puteoli assist Paul after his arrival?

What did some of the believers in Rome do to welcome Paul?

Upon Paul's arrival in Rome, how might the believers there have assisted him?

Give some examples of how fellow believers have helped to guide you in making decisions related to housing, work, or education.

8

Our Journeys in Guidance

For the past seven chapters we have surveyed the journeys of Paul recorded in Acts and discovered twenty lessons in them connected to divine guidance. Luke chronicles approximately three decades of Paul's life beginning with his conversion on the road to Damascus to his house arrest in Rome. Throughout the thousands of miles of travel by land and sea, Paul is portrayed as a minister of Jesus Christ whose steps have continually been guided by the Holy Spirit. And the ways that the Spirit said "Go" to him have been various.

These twenty lessons can be broken down into three categories: 1) supernatural, 2) volitional, and 3) providential. Each lesson with its number in parentheses has been placed in one of these categories.

1. Supernatural: Prophets (2), Closed Doors (10), Visions and Dreams (11), Personal Prophecy (16), and Angels (19).

2. Volitional: Spiritual Mentors (3), Church Leaders (4), Human Networks (5), Sense of Duty (8), Spirit-led Decision Making (13), Spirit's Compulsion (15), and Fellow Believers (20).

3. Providential: Sovereignty (1), Providential Encounters (6), Adversity (7), Conflict (9), Open Doors (12), Changed Circumstances (14), Religious, Civic, and National Identities (17), and Faulty Decision Making (18).

Category 1 is represented by five examples, Category 2 seven examples, and Category 3 eight examples. A presumption about divine guidance might be that Category 1, with its emphasis on the supernatural, would predominate. However, the fact that three categories exist shows the diverse and creative ways by which Paul was guided on his journeys. These twenty examples then are only suggestive of the varied approaches that the Spirit can use even today to guide believers as they go.

The titles for these lessons are somewhat subjective as well. You might assign a different title to some of them. And often the lesson involves a combination of ways of guidance such as an open and closed door, networking, dream or vision, or the counsel of church leaders, or suggestions by fellow believers.

Because this book's approach is inductive, it does not offer a checklist of principles for seeking guidance. Such checklists can be found in other books on guidance. Garry Friesen's general principles, mentioned in Lesson 13, may be useful for determining of God's will. While such an approach is sound and may be helpful for making major decisions, it tends to be cumbersome for most of life's decisions. Paul's example of living a life in the Holy Spirit, addressed repeatedly in his letters (e.g., Gal 5:16, 25; Rom 8:4–5), allows for a more dynamic view of guidance. This is the pattern we have also seen in Acts. Walking in the Spirit ensures being guided by the Spirit.

Dindy and I jokingly say that it was probably good that we met before we became Christians; otherwise, we might never have gotten together. It is likely that a personality checklist, like those used in Christian counseling or on an Internet dating site, would never have matched our profiles. When I saw Dindy across the tipi during the peyote meeting in Colorado, I was immediately attracted to her. I soon discovered that my attraction was more than physical but intellectual and spiritual as well. Most of our decisions have this intangible element. We use the expression "gut feeling" to describe the inexpressible, instinctual element that something is right or wrong. As followers of Christ, that sense is now under divine control so we might call it a "Spirit feeling." In closing, let me encourage you to listen to the Spirit as he directs you to "Go!" With trust and confidence you can make the decisions necessary for spiritual success throughout your own journey in life.

APPENDIX 1

Additional Examples of Guidance in Acts

Peter received a word of wisdom that David had prophesied about filling Judas' vacant place, so the apostles chose Matthias by casting lots (1:15–26).

Peter and John had a providential encounter with the lame beggar on their way to prayer at the temple and healed him (3:1–10).

Because of preaching in the temple, Peter and John were arrested, and through this adversity they were guided to speak the gospel before the Sanhedrin (4:1–21).

Because of faulty decision making, Ananias and Sapphira lied to the apostles and to the Holy Spirit and were struck dead (5:1–10).

The apostles were arrested in Jerusalem, and that night an angel opened their prison doors and directed them to continue preaching in the temple courts (5:12–20).

Because of a sense of duty to distribute food equally to the Greek and Hebrew widows, the disciples choose seven men full of the Spirit to oversee the food service (6:1–6).

Changed circumstances in Jerusalem after Stephen's martyrdom scattered many believers to Judea and Samaria, and Philip overcame his Jewish prejudice to preach successfully to the Samaritans (8:4–7).

Peter and John were sent to Samaria by the church leaders in Jerusalem to pray for the Holy Spirit to fall on the Samaritans (8:14–17).

An angel directed Philip to go to the Gaza road (8:26), and once there the Holy Spirit directed him to speak to the Ethiopian eunuch (8:27–30).

After baptizing the eunuch, Philip was taken by the Spirit to Azotus and nearby towns to continue preaching (8:38–40).

An angel appeared to Cornelius in Caesarea directing him to send messengers to Joppa to summon a man called Peter (10:1–8).

Peter concurrently received a vision three times of unclean food that prepared him to go with Cornelius' messengers and enter the home of a Gentile (10:9–23; cf. 11:4–17; 15:7–11).

The prophet Amos provided guidance to James for the word of wisdom that he shared concerning Gentile believers at the council in Jerusalem (15:15–21).

Appendix 2

From Peyote Way to Jesus Way

Dindy grew up in a Jewish family on the Upper West Side of New York City. Although she and her sister were not strictly brought up, the family religiously celebrated Passover each year at her observant aunt's house. Her father, who practiced his faith more than her mother, attending a western Sephardic Spanish and Portuguese synagogue occasionally. An early memory about Jesus occurred during her teen years. During a visit to the Metropolitan Museum of Art she bought a print of Rembrandt's head of Christ because she thought his face was so kind and caring. Later her father came into her bedroom and saw the print hanging on the wall. He ordered her to take it down immediately because it was unacceptable to display a picture of Jesus in their Jewish home. After college and a failed marriage Dindy later found herself in California with a young daughter Leilani. With some friends she spent two months in Hawaii as part of a film directed by Chuck Wein that starred Jimi Hendrix. "Rainbow Bridge" was the result, and she made several cameo appearances in the movie. A vivid memory for her was listening to Jimi practice his guitar for several hours on the grounds of the Catholic school where they were staying on Maui.

Contrarily, I grew up in two small North Dakota towns, Fullerton and Enderlin, where my family always attended church. I sang in the church choir and was a member of the Methodist Youth Fellowship (MYF) in Enderlin, where I graduated in a class of fifty. However, by my late teens I had rejected Christianity and become an agnostic. While a student at Hamline University in the Twin Cities, I began to explore the counter-cultural world of drugs, sex, and rock-n-roll. Then in 1968 I dropped out to become involved in the anti-Vietnam War movement and subsequently became a conscientious objector.

In 1969 I moved to Arcata, California, where I began to experiment with hallucinogenic drugs as a religious experience. I also became interested in American Indian culture. While returning from New York on a cross-country trip, I stopped in the Huerfano Valley in southern Colorado to visit several communes where hippies were using peyote in a ritual way. Considering this the perfect fusion of Indian culture and hallucinogenic drugs, I decided to relocate there.

In the spring of 1971 I packed up and headed to Colorado to join a commune called the Red Rocks. Twenty adults plus children lived in a sixty-foot geodesic dome. Some members were attending peyote meetings while others were involved in I Ching, Eastern religions, and various other New Age and occult activities.

Dindy relocated to Colorado around this same time and took up residence with her two daughters at the Triple A commune living first in a tipi and later in a tent. We each decided to attend a peyote meeting at another commune called Libre, and there I first saw Dindy on the other side of the fire across the tipi. After the meeting I introduced myself, and a relationship quickly developed. Soon we began to live together at the Red Rocks, and I became the instant father of Leilani and Winema.

We were both religious seekers and desired to become more involved in the Native American Church, the legal name of the peyote cult. After a brief sojourn near Taos, New Mexico, we were invited by Lakota Sioux friends to come and live on the Pine Ridge Reservation. After the events of Wounded Knee were resolved in 1972, we moved to nearby Porcupine to reside near the high priest of the NAC in South Dakota. I became his disciple, and our lives now revolved around attending weekly Saturday night peyote meetings. In the meantime our closest friends from the Red Rocks commune, Jim and Stephanie Ansen, had become believers and began to witness to us. We drove to New Mexico to attempt to win them back to the "peyote way." At the time we listened constantly to peyote music taped in the meetings, so we kept the music going during our drive south. We stopped in Denver for lunch and put the tape recorder in the rear window. Upon our return we were surprised to find that it had melted, so we threw the tape recorder into a trash can! That ended our listening to peyote music! Also, Jim was a chain smoker who rolled his day's supply of cigarettes every morning. I told Dindy that if Jim had truly changed and become a

Christian, a sign for me would be that he had quit smoking. Upon our arrival Jim greeted us at the front door with his usual big smile and said, "Guess what? I've stopped smoking!" Needless to say, that got my attention.

During a peyote meeting around this time I experienced the unsettling event described in Appendix 3, "The Night I Met the Devil." Later another piece of the puzzle was revealed after we became believers. We met a woman also named Dindy (Virginia) who was serving with her husband Ray as Wesleyan missionaries among the Lakota Sioux. Dindy mentioned to Dindy that she had seen us in times past on the reservation and had prayed for us thinking, "They really need God!" God was truly up to something, but we still couldn't see the final spiritual picture.

Early in 1974 Dindy's divorce was finalized, we got married on March 4, and our son James was born on March 26. The Holy Spirit was orchestrating a rapid series of events that would soon culminate in our salvation on Mother's Day. That decision to follow Jesus required us to move out of the NAC House in Potato Creek, where we served as its custodians. We moved back to Porcupine and began to attend the Mennonite Brethren Church there.

We had been living off Dindy's small inheritance, and our expenses had been minimal. But then the Holy Spirit spoke something to me: "Get a job." For a former hippie whose goal had been to live off the land by hunting and foraging, this was pretty radical. Because there were few jobs on the reservation, in early 1975 we moved to nearby Chadron, Nebraska. And I got a job—as a janitor's assistant cleaning toilets and mopping floors at Chadron State University. It was a humble beginning but one born out of obedience and our commitment to follow the Lord's leading. As we look back at the events leading to our conversion in 1974, we are keenly aware of their sovereign orchestration by God.

Appendix 3

The Night I Met the Devil

In 1974 events occurred that transformed the lives of Dindy and me. These happened through the witness and prayers of many people, most notably my mother Marilyn. She never met Dindy because she died prematurely in the summer of 1972. Yet her letters and prayers before her home-going were instrumental in our transformation. It is fitting then that on Mothers' Day 1974 Dindy and I became spiritual twins born again into the kingdom of God. It is to the memory of my mother that I would like to dedicate this account of the miraculous spiritual journey the Lord has brought us through.

The winter of 1973 found us with our two children Leilani and Winema living in the Badlands of southwestern South Dakota at Potato Creek, a remote community of Oglala Sioux on the Pine Ridge Indian Reservation. Our home was a log meeting house of the Native American Church—the peyote cult.

A Comanche chief, Quanah Parker, originated the religious use of peyote in the late 1800s. While on his deathbed in Texas, Parker was given an herbal remedy prepared by a Mexican woman. The herb was peyote. While under its influence, Parker heard a voice telling him: "Take this herb back to your Indian people, for it will be a source of comfort and strength to them." The Plains Indians at that time were a defeated people. They had lost their land; their culture and religion had nearly been destroyed. A great spiritual and psychological vacuum existed among Native Americans. Christianity was beginning to fill that void. But peyotism soon spread like wildfire and deterred any significant gains by missionaries.

What is this peyote that produced Parker's vision and has caused legal controversy until today? Peyote is a hallucinogenic cactus whose principal alkaloid is mescaline. It grows only in the Rio Grande valley of Texas and northern Mexico. As a sacrament of the NAC, peyote is legally recognized by the federal government and many states. Licensed dealers may harvest the cactus and sell it to church members, either in person or through the mail. But for nonmembers, peyote is still an illegal drug whose possession carries stiff penalties. Eating the bitter cactus often causes vomiting. For users, however, there is little danger of addiction and no long-term physically addictive effects.

The Winnebago and Omaha tribes introduced peyote to the Sioux in the early 1900s. Unlike Oklahoma tribes such as the Cheyenne and Arapaho who deemphasized any Christian elements, the Sioux blended Christianity into their peyote worship. They viewed tobacco smoking during times of prayer as sinful and thus dropped its use. The Half Moon altar, central to the worship ceremony, was modified to include a cross through its center. The chief peyote—a fetish-like dried peyote—was placed on a Bible at the head of the altar. The two then become the focus of worship during the services. New member were baptized by sprinkling with water. During the meetings sermons were preached that extolled morality, salvation through Christ, and heaven and hell.

Nevertheless, the main attraction is still peyote. Throughout the nightlong services it is consumed in great quantities, either green, dried, or drunk as tea. Its use is justified biblically by appeals to Paul's words in Romans 14:2: "Another, who is weak, eateth herbs" (KJV). Church members believe that eating peyote strengthens their weak faith. The peyote songs have no meaning linguistically but are spiritual songs sung to Wakantanka (God). The music, the worshipers claim, is the NAC equivalent of speaking in tongues. As participants consume more peyote, the Great Spirit often gave an "interpretation" to these otherwise meaningless syllables, something that I too have experienced.

My first encounter with peyote came on a hippie commune in southern Colorado in 1971. I had been involved in Eastern religion, occultism, and hallucinogenic drugs, so was eager to experiment with American Indian worship. A one-legged Arapaho Indian from Oklahoma was teaching hippies the "peyote way." It was in a tipi high in the Sangre de Christo range of the Rocky Mountains that I met Dindy. We began to attend meetings together throughout the Southwest. Interestingly, the strong ethical demands of the movement began to change our lifestyle. Indian members told us, for the privilege of using peyote, we needed to stop using drugs and clean up our act. And the men had to cut their long hair. God thus used the peyote church to pre-evangelize many hippies who later came to Christ.

Near Denver we had our first encounter with Sioux Indians who worshipped with the Cross Fire altar, described above. At first I was put off by the Christian elements in their meetings. I had grown up in a Mainline Protestant denomination and had totally rejected its version of Christianity by my late teens. I did not want to even *hear* the name of Jesus. Little did I know that the Holy Spirit was using this to soften my heart. In 1972 we were invited to South Dakota to visit the land and the people later made famous by the Academy Award-winning movie "Dances with Wolves." The many Lakota friends we made invited us to move onto the reservation. This decision was interrupted in 1973 by the three-month occupation of Wounded Knee, an act of protest carried out by the American Indian Movement. After its resolution on May 8, our family moved from Taos, New Mexico, to Pine Ridge in our old Chevy pickup. We soon were among the first whites ever to become baptized members of this all-Indian church. Faithfully we began to attend meetings on reservations all across South Dakota.

On a winter evening in 1974, the peyote meeting convened at the Potato Creek church house in which we lived. It was a funeral meeting for a young man who had been stabbed to death during a drunken brawl. His parents, though backslidden peyote members, still wanted a church funeral. The night was dark and freezing cold so only a handful of members were present. I sat on a pillow along the south wall of the church. Across from me sat Tom, one of the church's old-timers and the uncle of the slain man.

Much peyote was eaten that night—at least fifty per person. Near the middle of the night the beaded staff passed to Tom; it was his turn to sing. To his right a drummer accompanied him with a rapid beat on a deer-hide stretched across a cast-iron water drum. Tom took up the gourd rattle and sang:

> Ah hey ney, heya wanna hey nu,
> Ah hey ney, heya wanna hey nu . . ..

Emotion gripped his voice as he mourned the loss of his nephew. His third song startled me: it was not a peyote song. The song seemed to be a traditional Lakota death song. Suddenly I became aware of a presence entering the room to my right.

Up to this point I sincerely believed that true worship of God existed in the NAC. I had seen significant healings occur in the meetings when the peyote, called *pezhuta* in Lakota meaning "medicine," was eaten. Prayer was regularly offered during the meetings, and the songs were about Jesus and his salvation through the peyote way. One thing did bother me though. A great love existed among the church members while under the influence of peyote. However, once its effects had worn off, jealousy, anger, and strife returned. Humanity's basic sin nature remained unchanged by eating peyote.

Through the doorway that night came something that I sensed was evil. As I watched "in the spirit," a single thought was impressed on my mind: "This is the devil coming to claim the soul of the dead man." As "it" moved across the room in front of me toward the casket near the altar, I could watch no longer. My body began to shake uncontrollably with the greatest fear ever to grip my life. Just when the devil left the room, I cannot say. My shaking finally subsided, but for the rest the meeting I felt weak and helpless. The next morning I described my experience to an Indian friend who was a longtime church member. He gave me a knowing look and refused to talk about it. God had rolled back the veil of the spiritual world and shown me the dark side of peyote.

That night triggered a chain of circumstances that would cause Dindy and me to leave the church and follow Jesus a few months later. Our conversion took place on Mothers' Day 1974. The night I met the devil proved crucial to my spiritual transformation. Before it, I had full confidence that the peyote way was a viable path to God. My vision of the devil had shaken that confidence. So I decided to exchange the spirit of an inanimate plant for the Spirit of the living God. Even though peyote may be legally recognized as the sacrament of the NAC, I discovered that theologically it is not a way to God. For Jesus' words were realized in my experience, "I am the way and the truth and the life. No one comes to the Father except through me" (John 14:6).

APPENDIX 4

The Fountainhead Prophecy
by Dick Eastman

"God spoke to me and told me that I had come to a fountainhead church, and I was to declare what that meant. A fountainhead, by definition, is 'the principal source.' Another definition is 'a place where rivers begin to flow.'

God is looking for churches where rivers of life flow from them. What I'm talking about is life that begins to flow on every occasion, because God is doing great things. A fountainhead church is one where there's a spirit of praise, where there's a spirit of prayer and involvement in spiritual warfare. A fountainhead church is a church that has a spirit of release. The more a church becomes a fountainhead, by the very nature of the river flowing out from the people, they become givers. They begin to support; they be-gin to stand behind efforts; they begin to send people to the ends of the earth. They either go, or they send or they pray. They're goers; they're giv-ers; they're pray-ers. Everybody becomes involved because there's a spirit of release.

There is one other thing that I need to tell you that a fountainhead church is. Someone surveyed the top 100 churches in the U.S. known for growth. One continuing thread that could be woven through all of them was risk. In every case they were willing to step out and do unbelievable things where others were not. We need to have that spirit of risk. God is looking for fountainhead churches to rise up and stand against the darkness."
Delivered at Kempsville Presbyterian Church, Sunday, April 13, 1986

APPENDIX 5

Prophecy Today

Growing up in a denominational Protestant church (Methodist), I had never heard any teaching about prophecy and the other gifts of the Holy Spirit. But in our spiritual journey before salvation, Dindy and I had experienced a great deal of supernatural activity. Dindy for a time practiced a healing method called Johrei and used it on many people including Jimi Hendrix. Both of us had used hallucinogenic drugs during our spiritual searching, which led us to use peyote with the American Indians. During our time in the Native American Church we witnessed supernatural speech as well as physical healings. The healing properties of peyote are suggested by its Lakota Sioux name, *pezhuta*, which means "medicine."

Aware of the supernatural world during our pre-Christian explorations, we were open after our conversion to discover the Spirit's gifts including prophecy. We thought that if Satan had such counterfeit gifts, how much more beneficial and powerful were the gifts that the Holy Spirit gave! So we began to attend Pentecostal and Charismatic churches that allowed the various manifestations of the Spirit. I have many friends who hold to a "cessationist" theological position regarding the gifts. However, my reading of Scripture along with my spiritual experience puts me in the "continuationist" camp, the term with which Sam Storms identifies himself. So I agree to disagree with my brothers and sisters who do not believe the gifts are for believers today. However, I urge them to refrain from calling the present operation of the gifts as "of the devil." As Dindy and I have learned from our spiritual journey, the devil's so-called "gifts" bear very different fruit from those produced by the genuine gifts of the Holy Spirit.

Bibliography

Burkhardt, Nadin, and Mark Wilson, "The Late Antique Synagogue in Priene: Its History, Architecture, and Context." *Gephrya* 10 (2013) 166–96.

Carswell, Jonathan. *Married to a Martyr*. Bletchley, UK: Authentic Media, 2009.

Davis, Thomas W., and Mark Wilson. "The Destination of Paul's First Journey: Asia Minor or North Africa?" *Pharos Journal of Theology* 97 (2016) 1–14.

Friesen, Gerry. "Principles for Decision Making—Overview." http://www.gfriesen.net/sections/willofgod_principles.php.

Gee, Donald. *Studies in Guidance*. London: Victory, 1940.

George, Timothy. "My Own Pilgrim's Progress," *Christianity Today*, August 19, 2015. http://www.christianitytoday.com/ct/2015/july-august/my-own-pilgrims-progress.html?utm_source=ctdirect-html&utm_medium=Newsletter&utm_term=9480360&utm_content=376616914&utm_campaign=2013

Goodrich, Gregory. "Vision Issues after Brain Injury." Brainline Interview. http://www.brainline.org/content/2010/02/vision-issues-after-brain-injury-brainline-talks-with-dr-gregory-goodrich_pageall.html.

Holmes, Michael W., editor. *The Apostolic Fathers: Greek Texts and English Translation*. Updated ed. Grand Rapids: Baker, 1999.

Marshall, I. Howard. *Acts*. Grand Rapids: Eerdmans, 1980.

Roberts, Mark D. "God's Guidance for Christians in Conflict." http://www.patheos.com/blogs/markdroberts/series/gods-guidance-for-christians-in-conflict/.

Smith, M. Blaine. *Knowing God's Will: Finding Guidance for Personal Decisions*. 2nd ed. Downers Grove, IL: InterVarsity, 1991.

Storms, Sam. *Convergence: Spiritual Journeys of a Charismatic Calvinist*. Oklahoma City: Enjoying God Ministries, 2005.

Stutzman, Linford. *SailingActs: Following an Ancient Voyage*. Intercourse, PA: Good Books, 2006.

Thompson, Glen L., and Mark Wilson. "Paul's Walk to Assos: A Hodological Inquiry into its Geography, Archaeology, and Purpose." In *Stones, Bones and the Sacred: Essays from the Colloquia on Material Culture and Ancient Religion in Honor of Dennis E. Smith*, edited by Alan Cadwallader, 269–313. Atlanta: SBL, 2016.

———. "The Route of Paul's Second Journey in Asia Minor: In the Steps of Robert Jewett and Beyond." *Tyndale Bulletin* 67.2 (2016) 217–46.

Wilson, Mark. "Barnabas or Saul: Who is Describing Saul's Conversion in Acts 9:27?" *Scriptura* 114 (2016) 1–6.

Bibliography

———. "Cilicia: The First Christian Churches in Anatolia." *Tyndale Bulletin* 54.1 (2003) 15–30.

———. "The Ephesian Elders Come to Miletus: An Annaliste Reading of Acts 20:15–18a." *Verbum et Ecclesia* 34.1 (2013) 1–9.

———. "The Lukan Periplus of Saint Paul's Third Journey with a Textual Conundrum in Acts 20:15." *Acta Theologica* 36.1 (2016) 229–54.

———. "Paul: Bound in the Spirit for Jerusalem, Acts 20:22." In *Devotions on the Greek New Testament* edited by J. Scott Duvall and Verlyn D. Verbrugge, 54–55. Grand Rapids: Zondervan, 2012.

———. "Revelation 19.10 and Contemporary Interpretation." In S*pirit and Renewal: Essays in Honor of J. Rodman Williams*, edited by Mark Wilson, 191–202. Sheffield: Sheffield Academic Press, 1994.

———. Review of *The "We" Passages in the Acts of the Apostles*, by William Sanger Campbell. *Neotestamentica* 45.2 (2011) 360–62

———. "The Role of the Holy Spirit in Paul's Ministry Journeys." *Ekklesiastikos Pharos* 87 (2005) 76–95.

———. "Saint Paul in Pamphylia: Intention, Arrival, Departure." *Adalya* 19 (2016) 229–50.

———. "Studies in Guidance: Donald Gee as an Interpreter of Saint Luke." *Australasian Pentecostal Studies* 18 (2016). http://aps-journal.com/aps/index.php/APS/article/view/9494.

———. "Syria, Cilicia, and Cyprus." In *The World of the New Testament: Cultural, Social, and History Contexts*, edited by Joel B. Green and Lee Martin McDonald, 498–500. Grand Rapids: Baker, 2013.

———. *The Victor Sayings in the Book of Revelation*. Eugene: Wipf & Stock, 2005.

———. "Was Paul a Cilician, a Native of Tarsus: A Historical Reassessment?" *Olba* VIII (2003) 93–107.

Williams, J. Rodman. "Angels on Assignment." https://www.cbn.com/spirituallife/BibleStudyAndTheology/DrWilliams/ART_angels.pdf.

Witherington, Ben. *The Acts of the Apostles*. Grand Rapids: Eerdmans, 1998.